Focus On English©
Reference Series
Making the difficult parts of learning English easy!
Beyond Phrasal Verbs:
Mastering Phrasal Verbs in Context for ESL Learners

© Copyright 2008 by Thomas A. Celentano

All rights reserved.
No part of this book may be reproduced in
any form without the express written
permission of the copyright holder.

All inquiries should be addressed to:

Focus On English
P.O. Box 1554
Kailua, Hawaii 96734
http://www.FOEBooks.com

ISBN 978-0-557-01911-3

Dedicated to my friend Ann Holway.

Focus on English© Mini Series Books
Making the difficult parts of learning English easy

Beyond Phrasal Verbs:
Mastering Phrasal Verbs in Context for ESL Learners

Efficient and ubiquitous, English phrasal verbs provide the ESL learner with a window onto the world of fluent English communication. Found in English idioms of all descriptions, the ESL learner who masters phrasal verbs will have access to vast areas of every day English communication. Much of informal English expression, slang, and jargon are structured around phrasal verbs.

This Focus on English© book not only contains a comprehensive listing of common English phrasal verbs, but also goes to lengths to explain meanings and variations of usage, including slang and informal expressions. The student will find clear, simple, explanations for each of the phrasal verbs, followed by examples of their correct usage in a sentence.

There is a Focus on English© mp3 audio book version of this book (available separately from www.FOEBooks.com), which is a convenient way for students on the go to maintain their study of this topic while traveling. If the student has the Focus on English© audio book that accompanies this book, then he or she will find that each of the examples will be read twice to allow for speaking practice. This method helps the student remember the lesson more easily and also helps the student with pronunciation.

Table of Contents

Using English phrasal verbs correctly, with explanations and examples

- **Chapter 1:** Phrasal verbs beginning with the letters A and B . . . 1

  - aim at, 2
  - ask for, 2
  - ask out, 2
  - ask over, 3
  - back down, 3
  - back off, 3
  - back up, 4
  - beat up, 4
  - beef up, 4
  - believe in, 5
  - bite off, 5
  - blow away, 5
  - blow off, 6
  - blow out, 7
  - blow up, 7
  - boil down to, 7
  - break down, 8
  - break in, 9
  - break off, 9
  - break out, 10
  - break through, 10
  - break up, 11
  - bring back, 11
  - bring over, 11
  - bring up, 12
  - brush up, 12
  - brush off, 12
  - build in, 13
  - bump into, 13
  - burn down, 13
  - burn up, 14
  - burst out, 14
  - butt in, 15

Table of Contents

- **Chapter 1** REVIEW . . . 15

- **Chapter 2:** Phrasal verbs beginning with the letter C . . . 18

  - call back, 19
  - call in, 19
  - call off, 20
  - call up, 20
  - calm down, 21
  - care for, 21
  - carry on, 21
  - carry out, 22
  - catch on, 22
  - catch up, 22
  - cheat on, 23
  - check in, 24
  - check out, 24
  - chop up, 24
  - clean out, 25
  - clear up, 25
  - clog up, 25
  - close off, 26
  - come across, 26
  - come along, 26
  - come apart, 27
  - come back, 27
  - come down, 28
  - come down with, 28
  - come from, 29
  - come in, 29
  - come off, 30
  - come on, 30
  - come out, 31
  - come through, 31
  - come up, 32
  - come up with, 32
  - con into, 33
  - con out of, 33
  - cool off, 33
  - count in, 34

Table of Contents

- count on, 34
- count up, 34
- cover up, 35
- crack down, 35
- cross off, 36
- cut back, 36
- cut down, 36
- cut off, 37
- cut out, 38
- cut up, 38

- **Chapter 2 REVIEW . . . 38**

- **Chapter 3:** Phrasal verbs beginning with the letters D, E, and F . . . 41

- deal with, 42
- do away with, 42
- do over, 43
- do without, 43
- dress up, 44
- drink down, 44
- drink up, 44
- drop in, 45
- drop off, 45
- drop out, 45
- dry off, 46
- dry out, 46
- dry up, 47
- eat up, 47
- eat out, 48
- empty out, 48
- end up, 49
- fall apart, 48
- fall behind, 49
- fall down, 49
- fall for, 49
- fall off, 50
- fall out, 50
- fall over, 51
- fall through, 52

vii

Table of Contents

- feel up to, 52
- fight back, 52
- figure on, 53
- figure out, 53
- fill in, 53
- fill out, 54
- fill up, 54
- find out, 55

- fix up, 55
- flip out, 56
- float around, 56
- follow through, 56
- follow up, 57
- fool around, 57
- freak out, 58

- **Chapter 3** REVIEW . . . 58

- **Chapter 4:** Phrasal verbs beginning with the letter G . . . 61

- get ahead, 62
- get along, 62
- get around to, 63
- get away, 63
- get back, 64
- get back at, 64
- get back to, 65
- get behind, 65
- get by, 65
- get down, 66

- get in, 66
- get off, 67
- get off on, 67
- get on, 68
- get out, 68
- get out of, 69
- get over, 70
- get over with, 70
- get through, 70
- get to, 71

Table of Contents

- get together, 71
- get up, 72
- give away, 72
- give back, 73
- give in, 73
- give out, 74
- give up, 74
- go about, 75
- go after, 75
- go ahead, 75
- go along with, 76
- go around, 76
- go away, 77
- go back, 77
- go back on, 77
- go beyond, 78

- go by, 78
- go down, 79
- go for, 79
- go in, 80
- go off, 80
- go on, 81
- go out, 82
- go over, 82
- go through, 83
- go up, 83
- go with, 84
- goof around, 84
- gross out, 84
- grow out (of), 85
- grow up, 85

- **Chapter 4 REVIEW** . . . 86

- **Chapter 5:** Phrasal verbs beginning with the letter H . . . 88

- hand back, 89
- hand in, 89

- hand out, 89
- hand over, 90

ix

Table of Contents

- hang around, 90
- hang on, 90
- hang out, 91
- hang up, 91
- have on, 91
- head back, 92
- head for, 92
- head off, 92
- head towards, 93
- hear about, 93
- hear of, 93

- heat up, 94
- help out, 94
- hit on, 94
- hold against, 95
- hold off, 95
- hold on, 95
- hold out, 96
- hold over, 96
- hold up, 97
- hook up, 97
- hurry up, 98

- **Chapter 5** REVIEW . . . 98

- **Chapter 6:** Phrasal verbs beginning with the letter K . . . 101

- keep at, 102
- keep away, 102
- keep down, 102
- keep from, 103
- keep off, 103
- keep on, 103
- keep to, 104

- keep up, 104
- kick back, 105
- kick out, 105
- knock off, 106
- knock out, 106
- knock over, 107
- know about, 108

Table of Contents

- **Chapter 6** REVIEW . . . 108

- **Chapter 7:** Phrasal verbs beginning with the letter L . . . 110

- lay down, 111
- lay off, 111
- lead up to, 112
- leave behind, 112
- leave off, 113
- leave out, 113
- let down, 113
- let in, 114
- let in on, 114
- let off, 114
- let out, 115
- let up, 115
- lie around, 116
- lie down, 116
- lift up, 116
- light up, 117

- line up, 117
- live with, 118
- lock in, 118
- lock out, 118
- lock up, 119
- look around, 119
- look at, 120
- look down on, 120
- look for, 121
- look forward to, 121
- look into, 121
- look out, 122
- look over, 122
- look up, 122
- look up to, 122
- luck out, 123

- **Chapter 7** REVIEW . . . 123

xi

Table of Contents

- ❑ **Chapter 8:** Phrasal verbs beginning with the letters M, N and O . . . 126

- make for, 127
- make of, 127
- make out, 128
- make up, 128
- mess up, 129
- mix up, 129
- move in, 130
- move out, 130
- narrow down, 130
- open up, 131

- **Chapter 8 REVIEW** . . . 132

- ❑ **Chapter 9:** Phrasal verbs beginning with the letter P. . .133

- pass on, 134
- pass out, 134
- pass over, 134
- pass up, 135
- pay back, 135
- pay for, 135
- pay off, 136
- pay up, 136
- pick on, 136
- pick out, 137
- pick up, 137
- pile up, 139
- piss off, 139
- plan ahead, 139
- plan for, 140
- plan on, 140
- play around, 140
- plug in, 141

xii

Table of Contents

- plug up, 141
- point out, 142
- point to, 142
- print out, 143
- pull off, 143
- pull out, 143
- pull over, 144
- pull through, 144
- punch in, 144
- punch out, 145
- put away, 145

- put back, 145
- put down, 146
- put in, 147
- put off, 148
- put on, 148
- put out, 149
- put past, 149
- put to, 150
- put together, 150
- put up, 151
- put up with, 152

- **Chapter 9 REVIEW** . . . 152

- **Chapter 10:** Phrasal verbs beginning with the letter R . . . 155

- rip off, 156
- rip up, 156
- rule out, 157
- run across, 157
- run around, 157

- run down, 158
- run into, 158
- run out, 159
- run over, 159
- run up, 160

- **Chapter 10 REVIEW** . . . 160

Table of Contents

❏ **Chapter 11:** Phrasal verbs beginning with the letter S . . . 162

- screw on, 163
- screw out of, 163
- screw up, 164
- see about, 164
- sell out, 165
- set out, 165
- set up, 166
- settle down, 166
- settle for, 167
- shake off, 167
- shake up, 168
- show off, 168
- show up, 169
- shut off, 169
- shut up, 170
- sign in, 170
- sign out, 171
- sign up, 171
- sit down, 171
- slip up, 172
- slow down, 172
- sneak in, 173
- sneak out, 173
- sort out, 174
- space out, 174
- stand around, 174
- stand for, 175
- stand up, 175
- start off, 176
- start out, 176
- start over, 177
- start up, 177
- stay off, 177
- stay out, 178
- stay up, 178
- step on, 179
- stick around, 179
- stick out, 179
- stick to, 180
- stick up, 180
- stick with, 181
- stop off, 182

Table of Contents

- stop over, 182
- straighten out, 183
- straighten up, 183
- stress out, 184
- switch off, 184
- switch on, 184

- **Chapter 11** REVIEW . . . 185

- **Chapter 12:** Phrasal verbs beginning with the letter T. . . 187

- take apart, 188
- take in, 188
- take off, 190
- take on, 191
- take out, 191
- take out (on), 191
- take over, 192
- Take to, 192
- take up, 193
- talk down (to), 194
- talk into, 194
- talk out of, 194
- tear down, 195
- tear off, 195
- tear up, 195
- tell apart, 196
- think about, 196
- think ahead, 197
- think over, 197
- throw away, 197
- throw out, 198
- throw up, 198
- track down, 199
- trade in, 199
- trick into, 200
- try on, 200
- try out, 200
- turn around, 201
- turn down, 201
- turn in, 202

Table of Contents

- turn into, 202
- turn off, 203
- turn on, 203
- turn out, 204
- turn over, 205
- turn up, 206

- **Chapter 12** REVIEW . . . 206

❏ **Chapter 13:** Phrasal verbs beginning with the letters U, W and Z . . . 209

- use up, 210
- wake up, 210
- warm up, 211
- wash off, 211
- wash up, 211
- watch out, 212
- wear down, 212
- wear off, 213
- wear out, 213
- wind up, 213
- wipe off, 214
- wipe up, 215
- work in, 215
- work out, 216
- work up, 216
- wrap up, 217
- write down, 218
- write up, 218
- zip up, 218

- **Chapter 13** REVIEW . . . 219

Chapter 1

*Phrasal verbs beginning with the letters **A** and **B***

In this and following sections you will learn how to use many different phrasal verbs correctly in a sentence.

There are two kinds of phrasal verbs, separable and inseparable. Separable phrasal verbs can take an object between the verb and the preposition. For example: *My father **picked** me **up** after school and drove me home.* Inseparable phrasal verbs cannot take an object between the verb and the preposition. For example: I asked my friends to **come along** with me to the Christmas party. ***Come along*** cannot be separated by an object.

The numbers in front of the examples that are in parenthesis (), correspond the to number of the explanation found directly above. So, for example: 1. *explanation* . . . refers to (1) *example* . . . . If there is only one explanation or meaning given for the phrasal verb, then there will be two examples given for the one explanation. Both examples will be marked with (1).

If you have the accompanying Focus on English mp3 audio book (available separately from the school store or from www.FOEBooks.com) listen to each of the phrasal verbs, followed by their meanings and then some examples of how they are used in real English sentences. Each example will be spoken twice. There will be a review at the end of this chapter.

Page 1

2

Phrasal verbs beginning with the letters A and B

Aim at *(separable)*: 1. To point something at something or someone; usually a gun or other weapon, as in this example: *The soldier **aimed** his rifle **at** the target.* 2. Intending to finish at a certain destination or goal, as in this example: *We're hoping to finish this evening. We're **aiming at** 8pm.*
  More examples:
  - (1) The man ***aimed*** the gun ***at*** the bank teller.
  - (2) The president of the company ***aimed at*** increasing his bank customers by 15%.

Ask for *(separable)*: 1. To request something from someone, as in this example: *I **asked** the waitress **for** the bill.* 2. To be due something, sometimes used to express consequence for something you did or did not do, as in this example: *Allan never insured his car. When he had an accident, he had to pay for the damage. He really **asked for** it.*
  More examples:
  - (1) The customer ***asked*** the store clerk ***for*** a box for her new dress.
  - (2) Bill lost all of his money gambling. He really ***asked for*** it when he bet all of his money in one night. (Meaning: he was really tempting bad luck when he decided to bet all of his money the way he did)

Ask out *(separable)*: 1. To invite someone to go somewhere (usually used in romantic situations), as in this example: *I **asked** the new girl in school **out** for dinner..*
  More examples:

- (1) My boyfriend *asked* me *out*. We are going to the movies tonight.
- (1) My sister told me that that new boy in the school *asked* her *out*.

Ask over (separable): 1. Usually used to invite someone to one's home, as in this example: *I asked my colleagues over for dinner on Friday.*
   More examples:
   - (1) Let's *ask* your teacher *over* for dinner Saturday night.
   - (1) My girlfriend *asked* me *over* to her house to meet her parents.

Back down (inseparable): 1. Means to give up; to shy away from, usually, some kind of challenge, as in this example: *The students wanted the teacher to change the exam date because the exam date was the same date as the concert. The teacher didn't back down.*
   More examples:
   - (1) We are not going to *back down*, we want a pay raise from the company or we will strike.
   - (1) My mother told me I couldn't go out this weekend. I argued with her but she didn't *back down*.

Back off (inseparable): 1. (informal) To stop being persistent, as in this example: *My sister asked my father many times if she could go to the concert. Finally, my father told her to back off and stop asking so much.* 2. To move away from in a reverse direction, as in this example: *The car backed off of the ferry.*
   More examples:

- (1) The police asked the girl many questions and she began to cry. When she began crying, the police *backed off* and stopped asking her questions.
- (2) Realizing she was walking on very thin ice, the girl carefully *backed off* the ice and onto land.

Back up (separable): 1. To move or go in reverse, as in this example: *The car **backed up** into the parking spot.*
More examples:
- (1) I had to *back* the car *up* to get out of my parking space.
- (1) Some of the students didn't understand Fedor's story, so he had to *back up* and tell some of it again.

Beat up (separable): 1. To subject someone or something to rough treatment, as in this example: *The thief tried to take the woman's purse, but the woman surprised him, **beat** him **up**, took his wallet, and then ran away — a most unfortunate day for the thief.*
More examples:
- (1) My friend really *beat up* the book that I lent him.
- (1) The gang of boys *beat up* the old man and then robbed him.

Beef up (separable): 1. To make stronger, more resilient, as in this example: *The soldiers had to **beef up** their fort against enemy attack.*
More examples:
- (1) We decided to make some changes to the motor in my car. We decided to *beef up* the motor so it would make the car go faster.

- (1) The leader of the country gave the order to *beef up* the military because he was afraid there might be an attack from a neighboring country.

Believe in (inseparable): 1. To have confidence in something or someone, as in this example: *If you **believe in** yourself and your abilities, you will be successful.*
  More examples:
  - (1) I did well on the exam because I *believed in* the idea that if I studied, I would do well on the exam.
  - (1) Many Hindus *believe in* Krishna, a deity worshiped across many traditions of Hinduism.

Bite off (inseparable): 1. To accept responsibility or work, or agree to do something; usually used when someone is agreeing to do more than normal, as in this example: *I **bit off** quite a bit when I agreed to do the project without help.*

  More examples:
  - (1) According to an old saying: Don't *bite off* more than you can chew. Meaning, don't accept or agree to more responsibility than you can actually accomplish.
  - (1) The student *bit off* quite a lot when he agreed to do the whole presentation by himself.

Blow away (separable): 1. To win by overwhelming odds, to impress in a very big way, as in this example: *The swimmer **blew away** the competition with a new world record.* 2. (informal) To kill, as in this example: *The drug dealers tried to **blow away** their rivals.* 3. To move something from one location to another via the wind or moving air, as in this example: *The hurricane **blew** the houses **away**.*

More examples:
- (1) We *blew away* the competition in that last soccer match! (Meaning they won by a large score.)
- (2) The gangsters *blew away* rival leader. (Meaning that they killed their rival).
- (3) The wind came up and *blew* the papers *away*. We had to run and catch them before they went into the street.

Blow off (separable): 1. (informal) To ignore a result, a in this example: *When Sally got home from shopping she discovered that the clerk did not give her the right change. She didn't worry about it; she blew it off because it was only five cents.* 2. To vent or release built up pressure, as in this example: *Sometimes Hiro goes to the gym to blow off the frustrations of the day.* 3. To remove with explosive force, as in this example: *The tornado blew the top off that building.*

More examples:
- (1) His boss yelled at him for loosing the sale, but he *blew* it *off* because his boss was having a bad day. (Meaning he ignored his boss' anger because his boss was not having a good day, which caused him to yell at his employees.)
- (2) He knew that his boss was just *blowing off* steam. (Meaning, he knew that his boss was suffering from stress and was yelling at people because of this stress.
- (3) The force of the explosion *blew off* the roof of the building.

Page 6

Blow out (*inseparable*): 1. To extinguish or be extinguished by wind or the force of moving air, as in this example: *The woman **blew out** the candle.* 2. To suddenly or abruptly stop working or fail, as in this example: *The switch **blew out** and now the washing machine doesn't work.*

More examples:
- (1) The wind came through the window and ***blew out*** the candles.
- (2) We ***blew out*** a fuse when we plugged in the oven.

Blow up (*inseparable or separable depending on usage*): 1. (*separable*) To explode with a bomb, to destroy something usually with explosives, as in this example: *The soldiers **blew up** the enemy trucks.* 2. (*inseparable*) To lose your temper; to have a discussion turn violent, as in this example: *Kaori **blew up** after learning that her boyfriend was dating another girl.* 3. (*separable*) To amplify, make something bigger, to enlarge, as in this example: *We **blew** the photograph **up** so we could see more details.*

More examples:
- (1) They ***blew*** the building ***up*** so they could build a new building on that location.
- (2) The men couldn't come to an agreement and one of them finally ***blew up*** (Meaning, one of the men finally got very angry.)
- (3) He really ***blew*** that story ***up***. That is not how it happened. (Meaning: he added things to the story that weren't true; he made they story sound more important than it really was.)

Boil down (to) (*inseparable or separable depending on usage*): 1. (*separable*) To reduce by boiling, as in this example: *My mother* made great chicken soup. She would **_boil_** a chicken **_down_** and then add vegetables. 2. (*inseparable*) To summarize (**_boil down to_**), as in this example: *What it **boils down to** is that we can't go on our vacation this year because of the airline strike.*

More examples:
- (1) The cook **_boiled_** the vegetables **_down_** until they were soft and then made a nice soup.
- (2) We have not been able to pay our bills and the demand for our products is getting smaller. What it **_boils down to_** is that our business is in trouble.

Break down (*inseparable or separable depending on usage*): 1. (*separable*) To divide into parts or pieces for analysis or in order to make repairs or upgrades, as in this example: *The scientists **broke** the problem **down** to try to understand it better.* 2. (*inseparable*) To suddenly collapse emotionally or physically; to become or cause to become upset or distressed, as in this example: *When the police told the suspected criminal that they knew he was guilty, he **broke down** and told them the truth.* 3. (*inseparable*) When something no longer functions; to become incapable of functioning, as in this example: *The car **broke down** at 2 o'clock in the morning and we had to wait until sunlight before we could get help.* 4. (*separable*) To eliminate, destroy, or abruptly remove a barrier, as in this example: *The police **broke down** the door to get inside the house.* 5. Used to mean weaken, reduce resistance to something, or cause to be ineffective, as in this example: *I didn't have enough money for a new car, but the salesman said it wouldn't be a problem. Eventually, I **broke down** and bought the new car with credit.*

More examples:
- (1) The mechanic is **_breaking down_** the engine to make a major repair.

- (2) When she heard of the accident involving her parents, she *broke down* and cried.
- (3) The car was *broken down* on the side of the road.
- (4) Don't be afraid to *break down* the barriers that prevent you from being successful.
- (5) I asked my mother many times if I could go to the rock concert. She finally *broke down* and let me go.

Break in(to) (separable): 1. To acclimatize something or someone to a task or action, as in this example: *The manager broke in the new employee, explaining to her the rules and procedures of their office.* 2. To enter an area or building by force, as in this example: *We forgot our keys and had to break into own house in order to get in.*

More examples:
- (1) It is important to *break* a new horse *in* before racing it. (Meaning: to help the horse become accustomed to its new job and surroundings.)
- (2) The robber *broke into* the house and stole the painting.

Break off (separable): 1. To stop something that was ongoing; to quit doing something, as in this example: *Our company broke off relations with the company from New York.* 2. To separate something from another thing by twisting or tearing, as in this example: Alex *broke off* a piece of bread and then ate it.

More examples:
- The couple decided to *break off* their wedding engagement because they decided they would not be happy together.

- The farmer ***broke off*** a branch of a tree and used it to make a mark on the ground.

Break out *(inseparable or separable depending on usage):* 1. *(informal) (separable)* To take something out for use; to cause something to appear suddenly, as in this example: *After hiking for two hours, we sat down under a tree,* ***broke out*** *a bottle of water and drank.* 2. To become infected with a disease, illness, or condition that is visible on the skin, such as red blotches or rashes, or pimples, as in this example: *The little girl's skin* ***broke out*** *in measles.* 3. *(inseparable)* To escape from, as in this example: *The hostages* ***broke out*** *of the room where they were being held and escaped.*

More examples:
- (1) Okay, let's ***break out*** the beer and begin this party! (Meaning, let's take the beer out of the cooler, refrigerator, or other location and let the party begin.)
- (2) Every student in the class ***broke out*** with a red rash. The doctor said it was not a serious disease.
- (3) The prisoner ***broke out*** of prison.

Break through *(inseparable):* 1. *(informal) (separable)* To advance or move through, usually suddenly and with force, some kind of barrier or obstacle, as in this example: *The rescuers broke through the wall to save the children in the burning building.*

More examples:
- (1) The miners finally ***broke through*** the hard rock and began digging their mine.
- (2) Aiko was having difficulty understanding the math problem. Finally, after hours of work, she ***broke through*** her misunderstanding and solved the problem.

Break up *(separable):* 1. *(separable)* To divide or separate into pieces or parts, as in this example: *We **broke up** the candy bar and gave a piece to the children.*
- **More examples:**
  - (1) The workers ***broke up*** the concrete sidewalk with their machine.
  - My father used to ***break up*** a cracker and put the pieces in his soup.

Bring back *(separable):* 1. To return something, as in this example: *I lent my friend my book and he **brought** it **back** this morning.* 2. To recall, as in memory, as in this example: *Seeing those students sitting in a classroom **brings back** the days when I was a teacher in high school.*
- **More examples:**
  - (1) The girl ***brought*** the music CD ***back*** after borrowing it from her friend for two weeks.
  - (1) The old man would like to ***bring back*** the days when life was simple.

Bring over *(separable):* 1. To carry or move something to a specific location, usually a location that is close to the speaker, as in this example: *Would you **bring** the pencil **over** here please.*
- **More examples:**
  - (1) Please ask Kaori to ***bring*** her CD ***over*** so we can listen to it. (Meaning, ask Kaori to bring her CD to this location.)
  - (1) Son, would you ***bring*** that tool ***over*** here, please. (Meaning, bring that tool to my location.)

Page 11

Bring up (separable): 1. To raise, as with a child or pet, as in this example: *I was born in New York, but I was **brought up** in California.* 2. To introduce into a discussion, as in this example: *During our discussion about grades, the teacher **brought up** the subject of homework.*

More examples:
- (1) The couple ***brought up*** two children, a girl and a boy.
- (2) *During a meeting:* I would like to ***bring up*** a question. When are we going to get a paycheck?

Brush up (inseparable): 1. To review something for the purpose of becoming familiar with it again, as in this example: *In order to get my driver's license, I had to **brush up** on my driving skills again.*

More examples:
- (1) I need to ***brush up*** on my Mandarin Chinese before we travel to China.
- (1) Students should ***brush up*** on the rules for taking exams before taking an important exam.

Brush off (separable): 1. To wipe something off of the surface of something else, as in this example: *The man lifted himself off of the ground, **brushed off** his jacket and walked away.* 2. To not be affected by something, as in this example: *Julian lost his job, but he didn't worry about it. He just **brushed** it **off** and looked for a new job.*

More examples:
- (1) The lady tried to ***brush*** the lint ***off*** of her dress before going to the party.

- (2) When I was learning to ski I would fall down frequently. I just _brushed_ it _off_ and continued to practice until I got good.

Build in (separable): 1. To construct something integral to or inside of something else; to have one thing be a part of and in close working relationship to another, as in this example: *The fan was **built into** the computer to keep the computer cool during operation.*
   More examples:
   - (1) That stove had an exhaust fan **_built in_**.
   - (1) The electrician **_built_** the electrical outlet **_into_** the wall.

Bump into (inseparable): To meet by surprise, as in this example: *I **bumped into** my teacher while I was in town.* 2. To run into lightly, as in this example: *I **bumped into** one of the other passengers while on the bus.*
   More examples:
   - (1) I **_bumped into_** my friend at the mall. (Meaning, I met my friend at the mall by surprise.)
   - (2) There was a lot of traffic and the white car **_bumped into_** the red one in front of it at the traffic light. (Meaning, the white car lightly hit the red one in front of it.)

Burn down (separable): 1. To raze; to destroy by fire, as in this example: *The store **burned down**, but fortunately all of the customers and employees escaped without injury.*
   More examples:
   - (1) The house next door **_burned down_**. The family lost everything.

- ❑ (1) The firefighters had a difficult time putting out the fire in the building and the building finally *burned down*.

Burn up (separable): 1. To be destroyed by fire, as in this example: *My car burned up when the motor caught fire.* 2. To use up or deplete, as in energy, as in this example: *The runner burned up all of his energy running up the hill.* 3. To make angry, as in this example: *The driver of that car turned in front of me. Boy, that really burns me up!*

More examples:
- ❑ (1) I'm going to take the trash out in the back yard and *burn* it *up*.
- ❑ (2) That big SUV really *burns up* the gas. (Meaning, the car really uses a lot of gasoline to operate.)
- ❑ (3) I was really *burned up* that I got such a low grade on the exam.

Burst out (inseparable): 1. To erupt suddenly (emotional), as in this example: *While watching the horror movie, my friend burst out with a scream during the scary part.* 2. To suddenly escape or exit from somewhere, as in this example: *When the little girl entered her bedroom, her brother burst out of the closet to try to scare her.*

More examples:
- ❑ (1) When she heard that she got a failing grade on the exam she *burst out* crying.
- ❑ (2) The policeman *burst out* the door in pursuit of the thief.

Butt in (inseparable): 1. To interrupt; an unwanted or unsolicited interruption, as in this example: *Can't you see that I am talking to this gentleman over here. Please don't **butt into** our conversation.*

More examples:
- (1) I was talking to my wife when you *butted in*.
  (Meaning: The person interrupted a conversation when he or she was not being spoken to.)
- (2) Please don't *butt in*; this is between Bill and me.
  (Meaning: Bill and I were having a discussion that didn't have anything to do with the other person.)

Chapter 1 review

*Phrasal verbs beginning with the letters **A** and **B***

Instructions: read and /or listen carefully to the sentences below. Fill in the blank spaces with the correct **preposition, particle,** or **adverb**. The answers can be found in this chapter (above).

1. The president of the company aimed ___ increasing his bank customers by 15%.
2. The customer asked the store clerk _____ a box for her new dress.
3. Please don't butt _____; this is between Bill and me.
4. When Martha heard that she got a failing grade on the exam she burst ____ tears.

5. That big American car really burns ___ gas.

6. The house next door burned _____. The family lost everything.

7. I bumped _____ my friend at the mall.

8. The girl brought the music CD _____ after borrowing it from her friend for two weeks.

9. Every student in the class broke _____ with a red rash. The doctor said it was not a serious disease.

10. The couple decided to break _____ their wedding engagement because they decided they would not be happy together.

11. It is important to break a new horse _____ before racing it.

12. The car was broken _____ on the side of the road.

13. We have not been able to pay our bills and the demand for our products is getting smaller. What it boils _____ ___ is that our business is in trouble.

14. He really blew that story _____. That is not how it happened.

15. The wind came through the window and blew _____ the candles.

16. The force of the explosion blew _____ the roof of the building.

17. The wind came ____ and blew the papers away. We had to run and catch them before they went into the street.

18. I did well on the exam because I believed ____ the idea that if I studied, I would do well on the exam.

19. My friend really beat ___ the book that I lent him.

20. I had to back the car ____ to get out of my parking space.

Chapter 2
Phrasal verbs beginning with the letter C

In this section you will learn how to use many different phrasal verbs that begin with the letter C correctly in a sentence.

There are two kinds of phrasal verbs, separable and inseparable. Separable phrasal verbs can take an object between the verb and the preposition. For example: *My father <u>**picked** me **up**</u> after school and drove me home.* Inseparable phrasal verbs cannot take an object between the verb and the preposition. For example: *I asked my friends to <u>**come along**</u> with me to the Christmas party.* <u>**Come along**</u> cannot be separated by an object.

The numbers in front of the examples that are in parenthesis (), correspond the to number of the explanation found directly above. So, for example: 1. *explanation . . .* refers to (1) *example . . . .* If there is only one explanation or meaning given for the phrasal verb, then there will be two examples given for the one explanation. Both examples will be marked with (1).

If you have the accompanying Focus on English mp3 audio book (available separately from the school store or from www.FOEBooks.com) listen to each of the phrasal verbs, followed by their meanings and then some examples of how they are used in real English sentences. Each example will be spoken twice. There will be a review at the end of this chapter.

There will be a review at the end of this chapter.

Phrasal verbs beginning with the letter C

Call back *(separable):* 1. To return a phone call, as in this example: *Kyoko **called** me **back** to confirm the date of the picnic.* 2. Request to return, as in this example: *The military commander **called** his men **back** from the battle.*

More examples:
- (1) I called the dentist but he didn't answer his phone. He ***called*** me ***back*** in about ten minutes.
- (2) The construction company ***called*** their men ***back*** after finding out that they could not do the job. (Meaning: The construction company asked its workers to return to the office because the company was unable to do the job that they had been requested to do.)

Call in *(separable):* 1. Request to assemble, as in this example: *The manager **called in** the workers for a meeting.* 2. To make a telephone call usually in a business or formal setting, as in this example: *Jon didn't feel well so he **called in** sick.*

More examples:
- (1) The military officer ***called in*** his best soldiers to fight the attackers.
- (2) The repairman ***called in*** his parts order to the warehouse.

Page 19

Call off (separable): To cancel or postpone, as in this example: *They **called off** the concert because of the bad weather.* 2. Request that someone or something stops doing something and returns, as in this example: *The military commander **called off** its troops because there was no longer a threat by the enemy.*

More examples:
- (1) The policeman ***called off*** his police dog after the thief surrendered. (Meaning, the policeman gave the dog the command to attack the thief. When the thief surrendered, then the policeman ordered the dog to stop attacking.)
- (2) ***Call off*** the picnic, it's going to rain. We'll postpone the picnic until next weekend.

Call up (separable): 1. To initiate a telephone call, as in this example: *I **called up** my sister in Kansas to discuss her wedding.* 2. To request to assemble, to summon, as in this example: *The government **called up** all of its soldiers to fight the war.*

More examples:
- (1) I ***called*** Janice ***up*** yesterday and asked her to lend me her history book.
- (2) The military is ***calling up*** all eligible young men to serve in the Army. (Meaning, The military is requesting that all young men who are physically able and are of a certain age to report to military headquarters for service.)

Calm down *(separable):* 1. To cause to become tranquil or calm, as in this example: *The storm had **calmed down** and the sun came out so we decided to go outside.*

More examples:
- (1) The man ***calmed down*** after the police recovered his wallet.
- (1) The children were nervous after hearing the explosion, so the teacher had to ***calm*** them ***down***.

Care for *(inseparable):* 1. To provide needed assistance or watchful supervision, as in this example: *The nurse **cared for** the patient.* 2. To indicate preference, as in this example: *My sister usually doesn't **care for** tomatoes.*

More examples:
- (1) The nanny ***cared for*** the children.
- (2) I don't ***care for*** that kind of food. I like Japanese food better.

Carry on *(separable):* 1. To continue without stopping, as in this example: *The teacher told the student to **carry on** doing the exercise for ten more minutes.* 2. To act or behave in an improper, excited or silly way, as in this example: *She **carried on** for a half an hour about how she was almost robbed in the city.*

More examples:
- (1) The lottery winner said that he would ***carry on*** working for his company.
- (2) When Kaori found out that she got the best grade in the class on the exam, she ***carried on*** for ten minutes.

Carry out *(separable)*: 1. Complete or finish something, as in this example: *The sales group carried **out** their mission to increase sales. Sales were up 25%.* 2. To follow or obey a command, order, or request, as in this example: *The commander of the military asked his soldiers to **carry out** his command.*
  More examples:
  - (1) The president of the company asked the manager if he could complete the project on time. The manager said that he could ***carry out*** the request without a problem.
  - (2) The police dog was expected to ***carry out*** the command of his trainer.

Catch on *(inseparable)*: 1. To understand, to learn, as in this example: *The German Shepherd dog is very smart. It **catches on** quickly and is easy to train.*
  More examples:
  - (1) The new worker ***caught on*** quickly.
  - (1) He was a smart student who could ***catch on*** quickly.

Catch up *(inseparable)*: 1. To come up from behind; overtake, as in this example: *The runner in second place **caught up** with the leader.* 2. When wrongdoings or mistakes are detected by someone else and then made known, as in this example: *The businessman didn't pay taxes for years, but the Tax Department finally **caught up** with him.* 3. To become involved with something, often unwillingly, as in this example: *As the sunset I got **caught up** in the beauty of the sky.* 4. To become up to date or current with something, as in this example: *I talked to my girlfriend yesterday to* **catch up** *with the latest gossip.*

More examples:
- (1) After thirty minutes, the racing car in 3rd place **caught up** with the leader.
- (2) I never studied in English class. When I took the exam I go a low grade. All of those weeks of not studying finally **caught up** with me. My parents were really mad.
- (3) The crowd was cheering every time our team played well. I got **caught up** in all of this excitement and began cheering with the crowd.
- (4) I was sick for two weeks and didn't go to school. My teacher gave me some homework assignments so that I could **catch up** with the rest of the class.

Cheat on (inseparable): To act dishonestly; to deceive by trickery; swindle, as in this example: *The business owner* **cheated on** *his tax form.* (Meaning: the business owner put the wrong income on his tax form so that he wouldn't have to pay everything he owed to the tax department.)

More examples:
- The student was caught **cheating on** the exam.
- Susan accused her boyfriend of **cheating on** her. (Meaning: Susan accused her boyfriend of dating another girl).

Page 23

Check in (separable): 1. To register, as at a hotel, as in this example: *When I **checked in** at 8:30am the clerk reminded me that checkout time was 12pm tomorrow.* 2. (*informal*) To contact someone for the purpose of confirming your presence, or exchanging information, as in this example: *I **checked in** with my parents to let them know where I was.*

   More examples:
- 1. We *checked in* at the hotel around 10pm.
- 2. I *checked in* with my colleagues to see if I could help with our project. (Meaning: I visited with my colleagues to find out if there was something I could do to help with the project.)

Check out (inseparable or separable depending on usage): 1. (*inseparable*) To settle one's bill and then leave, as at a hotel, as in this example: *We asked the hotel clerk if we could **check out** an hour later than normal.* 2. (*separable*) (*informal*) To scrutinize or look over carefully, as in this example: *We went to the mall to **check out** the sales.*

   More examples:
- (1) We *checked out* of the hotel at noon.
- (2) We decided to go to the auto showroom and *check out* the new BMWs.

Chop up (separable): 1. To cut into small pieces, as in this example: *We **chopped up** the tomatoes and made a nice salad.*

   More examples:
- (1) The cook *chopped up* the garlic and the onions and put them into a saucepan.

- (1) Then, the cook *chopped up* the beef and put that into the saucepan.

Clean out *(separable):* 1. To remove clutter or everything from a room or area; sometimes implies that the area is in critical need of cleaning, or that the area has to be made ready for another occupant by removing everything, as in this example: *I cleaned out my car because it was a mess.*
  More examples:
  - (1) I have to *clean out* my house to get ready for spring cleaning.
  - (1) They had to *clean out* the warehouse so that the new business could move in.

Clear up *(separable):* 1. To make free from doubt or confusion, as in this example: *I was confused about the test date, but the teacher cleared that up.* 2. When a disease condition heals and goes away, especially a skin condition, as in this example: *When I went back to the doctor I showed him that the rash had cleared up.*
  More examples:
  - (1) We have to *clear up* the misunderstanding between us. (Meaning: we have to have a discussion so that we can understand each other point of view better.)
  - (2) The rash *cleared up* after I took the medicine.

Clog up *(separable):* To obstruct movement on or in something; when obstructions (something that blocks an opening) prevent

something from working properly, as in this example: *The bathtub drain is **clogged up** and water won't drain out of the tub.*
  More examples:
  - (1) The sink drain is **clogged up**. Water will not pass out of the drain.
  - (1) The roads were all **clogged up** with traffic.

Close off *(separable):* 1. To block or obstruct an area, usually deliberately, so that something or someone cannot pass, as in this example: *Main Street was **closed off** to car traffic because of the street celebration.*
  More examples:
  - (1) The police **closed off** the main street because of the big parade.
  - (1) The workers **closed off** one of the entrances to the building because of construction inside the building.

Come across *(inseparable):* 1. To encounter or discover; to find unexpectedly, as in this example: *While traveling in China, I **came across** a man who was kind enough to show me the ancient temple.*
  More examples:
  - (1) The man **came across** some old photographs while searching through his closet.
  - (1) The workers **came across** some old coins while digging a hole in the ground.

Come along *(inseparable):* 1. To accompany; to go with someone, as in this example: *The mother told the child to **come***

along with her into the car. 2. To make progress, as in this example: *The company's new project was **coming along** nicely.*
More examples:
- (1) The tour guide told the tourists to *come along* with him so that he could show them some interesting things about the city.
- (2) The new building is really *coming along*. (Meaning: the construction on the new building is progressing very well.)

Come apart *(inseparable):* 1. To separate, to fall to pieces or fall apart because of poor condition or construction, as in this example: *Her old dress looked nice but it **came apart** when she tried to put it on.* 2. To lose control emotionally, as in this example: *When the man discovered that his wife was seeing another man, he **came apart**.*
More examples:
- (1) The old book *came apart* when I tried to open it.
- (1) When she found out that the school would not accept her she really *came apart*. (Meaning: she became emotionally upset when she found out the school would not accept her.)

Come back *(inseparable):* 1. To return, as in this example: *After going to the theater, Nancy came back home about 11:30pm.* 2. To have a consequence, as in this example: *Not doing your homework will **come back** to you in a bad way. Maybe you will do poorly on an exam.* (Note: we use come back to mean return in

Page 27

many ways. In this case it means: Your laziness will return to you when you take an exam and discover you don't know the answers.)

More examples:
- (1) Our daughter was away at school for two years. She *came back* yesterday.
- (2) The salesman's laziness *came back* on him when he was fired for a poor sales record.

Come down (inseparable): 1. Movement from a higher level to a lower level, as in this example: *He came down off of the ladder and stepped on the ground.* 2. Socially moving from a good position to a lesser position, as in this example: *Boy, I remember when she was a great actress. Now no one knows who she is. She has really come down.* 3. Business: when pricing is reduced, as in this example: *Clothing prices have really come down at the mall. Let's go shopping!*

More examples:
- (1) My friend from New York is *coming down* to visit me here in Florida.
- (2) Poor Ted, he's lost his job and now he has to move out of his apartment. Boy, he's really *come down*.
- (3) During the sale, the prices *came down*.

Come down with (inseparable): 1. To get sick, as in this example: *Many of the students in the same class came down with a cold.*

More examples:
- (1) My head is hot and my throat hurts, I think I am *coming down with* the flu.

- (1) While visiting Thailand, my friend *came down with* malaria.

Come from *(inseparable)*: 1. Origin; location where something or someone originated, as in this example: *He came from the south of the country.* 2. Can also be used to refer to a person's reference point when they are giving their opinion to another, as in this example: *Your boss seems mean and nasty, but you must understand where he is coming from.* The president of the company will fire your boss if your boss doesn't enforce the rules.

More examples:
- I just *came from* the grocery store. I bought some food for dinner tonight.
- In Mark's opinion, international aid should be sent to that nation. I think that he is *coming from* a place of compassion. (Meaning: the reason why he is saying this is because he feels compassion for the people of the poor nation.)

Come in *(inseparable)*: 1. To enter or to request or give permission to enter, as in this example: *Julia came in the front door soaking wet because of the heavy rain outside.* 2. Used to talk about including or inserting an idea, activity, event, etc., into an existing situation, as in this example: *We are planning an outdoor celebration. We are going to have food and competitions. The bike race will come in between the swimming race and the running race.*

More examples:

- ❏ (1) There is someone knocking at our door. It must be our dinner guests, please ask them to *come in*.
- ❏ (2) Getting good grades on exams takes hard work. This is where doing homework *comes in*.

Come off (inseparable): 1. To result in; to end up, as in this example: *If we don't sell our products more cheaply, we will come off the losers in this market.* 2. To happen or occur, as in this example: *The picnic came off perfectly because of the beautiful weather.* 3. To separate away from, as in this example: *The cover came off of that book.*

More examples:
- ❏ (1) If we don't score some points in this soccer match we are going to *come off* looking like a bad team.
- ❏ (2) The party *came off* poorly because there wasn't enough food.
- ❏ (3) The handle *came off* of the cheap cooking pot.

Come on (inseparable): 1. Request to accompany, motivational imperative, or used in the imperative to mean hurry up, as in this example: *Come on, we're going to be late for the movies!* 2. (slang) to show romantic or sexual interest in someone, as in this example: *The guy at the bar came on to me, but I wasn't interested.*

More examples:
- ❏ (1) *Come on* with me and I'll show you the office.
- ❏ (2) The guy looked like a movie star. All the girls at the party *came on* to him.

Come out *(inseparable):* 1. The results of; as in this example: *The total for all of the groceries **came out** to $52.* 2. First appearance, as in this example: *This fashion line of dresses **came out** last month.* 3. Make an appearance, as in this example: *The sky was clear and you could see the stars **come out**.* 4. Remove or come away from, as in this example: *Lots of sand **came out** of my pocket when I returned from the beach.*

More examples:
- (1) You blood test ***came out*** negative. You are not sick.
- (2) The book ***came out*** last week. It was really exciting.
- (3) It was a beautiful night. The moon ***came out***.
- (4) The dirt ***came out*** easily when she washed the soiled dress.

Come through *(inseparable):* 1. To pass (usually successfully) from the beginning to the end of an experience, as in this example: *The student **came through** the exam okay.* 2. To move from one place to another; pass by and then continue on to a destination; to pass under or between a structure on your way to somewhere, as in this example: *I knew a lot of people that **came through** that door.* 3. To be successful at completing something, or getting something done for someone else, as in this example: *I can always rely on my best friend to **come through** for me.*

More examples:
- (1) He ***came through*** a really bad experience. He was hospitalized after a bad car accident. But today he is finally well.

- (2) During our party, people that I didn't know *came through* the door
- (3) Our team won the championships. They *came through* for us.

Come up (inseparable): 1. Moving from a lower position to a higher position, physically or socially, as in this example: *He came up the stairs in a hurry. He was late for the meeting.* 2. New or unexpected appearance of an idea or event, as in this example: *A sudden storm came up and ruined our picnic.* 3. Anticipation of an event, holiday, or other situation, as in this example: *The Cherry Blossom celebration is coming up this week.*

More examples:
- (1) They *came up* to Canada from Texas to visit us.
- (2) Thank you for the invitation to your party. I'm sorry I can't go, something important has *come up*. (Meaning that an unexpected situation has arisen for the speaker.)
- (3) Christmas is *coming up* next week.

Come up with (inseparable): 1. To originate, to think of, to invent, as in this example: *Yolanda came up with a good idea. She would go to America with her friends to study English.*

More examples:
- (1) We need to *come up* with a some good ideas for the party next week.
- (1) Rudolf Diesel *came up* with the idea for the diesel engine.

Con into *(inseparable):* 1. Use a deceitful method to get someone to do something (💡Note: sometimes this expression is used playfully), as in this example: *My friends **conned** me **into** helping them clean up the house.*
- **More examples:**
  - ❑ (1) The woman was ***conned into*** sending money to an organization that did not exist.
  - ❑ (1) My boss ***conned*** me ***into*** doing the large project. (The speaker does not mean that his boss used negative trickery; only that his boss persuaded him to do a project that he hadn't planned to do.)

Con out of *(inseparable):* 1. Use a deceitful method to get something from someone. (💡Note: sometimes this expression is used playfully), as in this example: *My girlfriend **conned** me **out of** my last $20.*
- **More examples:**
  - ❑ (1) The phony advertisement on the Internet ***conned*** us ***out of*** our money.
  - ❑ (1) My wife ***conned*** me ***out of*** $50 for a new dress. (💡Note: The speaker does not mean that his wife used negative trickery; only that his wife persuaded him to give her money for the new dress.)

Cool off *(separable):* 1. To become more relaxed (usually after being upset), as in this example: *It took me two hours to **cool off** after the policeman gave me a ticket.* 2. To reduce temperature, as in this example: *It took me two hours to **cool off** after jogging in the sun.*

More examples:
- (1) After the argument, he left the room and tried to **cool off**. (Tried to become more calm)
- (2) After boiling the eggs, the cook left them out to **cool off**.

Count in *(separable):* 1. To include, as in this example: *My father asked us if we wanted to go to a nice restaurant tonight. I told him to **count** me **in**!*

More examples:
- (1) The project seemed interesting. I asked the group to **count** me **in**. (Meaning: I wanted to be included in the project.)
- (1) Who wants to have ice cream now? **Count** me **in**, I love ice cream!

Count on *(inseparable):* 1. To rely on, as in this example: *I could always **count on** my brother to help me when I was in trouble.*

More examples:
- (1) I knew that I could **count on** my friend to pick me up from work.
- (1) An employer likes to hire someone they can **count on**.

Count up *(separable):* 1. To tally; to add up, as in this example: *After the swap meet we **counted up** the money and discovered that we made over $500.*

Examples:
- (1) At the end of the day, the business *counts up* the amount of money it made.
- (1) We *counted up* the number of holidays we have every year.

Cover up (separable): 1. To hide something, to be blocked from view, as in this example: *I couldn't find my car keys because they were on the table covered up by my purse.*

More examples:
- The politician tried to *cover up* his connection to the criminal. (Meaning: the politician didn't want people to know he had a connection to a criminal)
- She put some makeup on to *cover up* the red marks on her face.

Crack down (inseparable): 1. To more strictly enforce law, order, or rules, sometimes suddenly, as in this example: *The school cracked down on smoking in the building.*

More examples:
- (1) The government *cracked down* on protesting in the city.
- (1) The company *cracked down* on lateness by employees. (Meaning: the company more strictly enforced the rules about being late to work.)

Cross off (separable): 1. To draw a line through; eliminate, as in this example: *I decided to **cross** my name **off** of the list of students who wanted to take the TOEIC exam.*

> **More examples:**
> - (1) She made a list of places that she wanted to visit. After she visited Rome, she *crossed* that city *off* of her list.
> - (1) My boss asked us to put our names on a list if we wanted a new position in the company. I hope they don't *cross* my name *off* of this list.

Cut back (separable): 1. To reduce; to make shorter or smaller, as in this example: *Because of the high price of petroleum, we had to **cut back** the amount of time that we were driving.*

> **More examples:**
> - (1) We were spending too much money so we had to *cut back* on spending.
> - (1) The company had to *cut back* on bus services because they weren't making enough money.

Cut down (separable): 1. To reduce; not use so much, as in this example: *It is important for farmers to **cut down** on the amount of pesticides that they use on our food.* 2. To remove by sawing or by using a knife or ax or other sharp tool, as in this example: *The bushes in my yard were too tall, so we **cut** them **down**.* 3. (informal) To ridicule, as in this example: *Tanya's friend really **cut** her **down** for being so mean to her boyfriend.*

> **More examples:**

- (1) We were spending too much money on our vacation so we had to *cut down* our spending.
- (2) They *cut down* the tree to make room for the new house.
- (3) Some of the students *cut down* the girl for wearing an old dress to school.

Cut off (separable): 1. To stop; discontinue, as in this example: *The government cut off aid to the poor.* 2. To move in front of someone or something else so as to interfere with their progress, as in this example: *The tall building directly in front of our window cut off our view of the ocean.* 3. To cut and completely remove with scissors or knife or other sharp instrument, as in this example: *The cook cut off the bad parts of the vegetables and threw them out.*

More examples:
- (1) His parents *cut off* his allowance because of his bad grades.
- (2) The car moved into the left lane and *cut off* the bus, which caused an accident.
- (3) The barber *cut off* Jim's hair. Jim had a bald head after visiting the barber.

Cut out (separable): 1. (informal) Leave unexpectedly, as in this example: *The students cut out a 2pm to go to a concert.* 2. To remove part of something like, for example, a section from a piece of paper with a scissors, as in this example: *The dressmaker cut out a sleeve from the cloth.* 3. To stop unexpectedly, as in this example: *The electric generator cut out and the city was without electricity for two hours.* 4. To stop using something, as in this example: *The doctor told me to **cut out** smoking because it wasn't good for my health.*

More examples:
- (1) The meeting was longer than expected so Stefan ***cut out*** early. (Means he left early)
- (2) The children ***cut out*** star shapes from the colored paper.
- (3) I was racing along the freeway when suddenly the car engine ***cut out*** and I had to turn the car off the road.
- (4) The woman was dieting so she cut out all sweets.

Cut up *(separable):* 1. Separate into pieces, usually with a knife or other sharp instrument, as in this example: *We **cut** the cake **up** into four equal pieces.* 2. *(informal)* To make jokes, as in this example: *My friends and I sat around the table and **cut up** all night.*

More examples:
- (1) The cook ***cut up*** the celery.
- (1) When my friends get together we always ***cut up***. (Meaning: we always make a lot of jokes.)

Chapter 2 review

Phrasal verbs beginning with the letter C

*Instructions: read and /or listen carefully to the sentences below. Fill in the blank spaces with the correct **preposition, particle,** or **adverb**. The answers can be found in this chapter (above).*

1. I called the dentist but he didn't answer his phone. He called me _____ in about ten minutes.

2. The repairman called ___ his parts order to the warehouse.

3. The children were nervous after hearing the explosion, so the teacher had to calm them _____.

4. The nanny cared ___ the children.

5. When Kaori found out that she got the best grade in the class on the exam, she carried _____ for ten minutes.

6. I don't care ___ that kind of food. I like Japanese food better.

7. The student was caught cheating ___ the exam.

8. We checked ___ at the hotel around 10pm.

9. We decided to go to the auto showroom and check ___ the new BMWs.

10. Then, the cook chopped ___ the beef and put that into the saucepan.

11. The project seemed interesting. I asked the group to count me ___.

12. The phony advertisement on the Internet conned us ____ of our money.

13. The government cracked _____ on protesting in the city.

14. She made a list of places that she wanted to visit. After she visited Rome, she crossed that city _____ of her list.

15. The company had to cut _____ on bus services because they weren't making enough money.

16. They cut _____ the tree to make room for the new house.

17. The car moved into the left lane and cut _____ the bus, which caused an accident.

18. The cook cut ____ the celery.

19. Some of the students cut _____ the girl for wearing an old dress to school.

20. The government cracked _____ on protesting in the city.

Chapter 3
Phrasal verbs beginning with the letters D, E, and F

In this section you will learn how to use many different phrasal verbs that begin with the letters D, E, and F correctly in a sentence.

There are two kinds of phrasal verbs, separable and inseparable. Separable phrasal verbs can take an object between the verb and the preposition. For example: *My father **picked** me **up** after school and drove me home.* Inseparable phrasal verbs cannot take an object between the verb and the preposition. For example: I asked my friends to ***come along*** with me to the Christmas party. ***Come along*** cannot be separated by an object.

The numbers in front of the examples that are in parenthesis (), correspond the to number of the explanation found directly above. So, for example: 1. *explanation . . .* refers to (1) *example . . . .* If there is only one explanation or meaning given for the phrasal verb, then there will be two examples given for the one explanation. Both examples will be marked with (1).

If you have the accompanying Focus on English mp3 audio book (available separately from the school store or from www.FOEBooks.com) listen to each of the phrasal verbs, followed by their meanings and then some examples of how they are used in real English sentences. Each example will be spoken twice. There will be a review at the end of this chapter.

Page 41

42

There will be a review at the end of this chapter.

Phrasal verbs beginning with the letters D, E, and F

___Deal with___ *(inseparable):* 1. To do business with, as in this example: *When we want to buy clothing we only __deal with__ the best stores.* 2. To interact with someone or something, as in this example: *The teacher always __dealt with__ his students in a fair way.* 3. *(separable)* To do what is necessary to solve a problem, as in this example: *The police always __deal__ harshly __with__ drug dealers.* 4. About or concerning, as in this example: *There is an excellent book on the environment. It __deals with__ the topic of global warming.*
   More examples:
   - (1) When we need laundry services we ___deal___ with Ajax Cleaners.
   - (2) When there was a problem between them, Marco always ___dealt with___ his wife in a compassionate way.
   - (3) My home had a leaky roof so I ___dealt with___ this problem by calling a roofing company.
   - (4) The newspaper article ___deals with___ the problem of drugs in big cities.

___Do away with___ *(inseparable):* 1. To end, as in this example: *The school __did away with__ the old system of grading students.* 2. To kill, as in this example: *The gangsters __did away__ with the rival leader.*
   More examples:

- (1) The teacher ***did away with*** homework in his classes.
(Meaning: the teacher no longer gave homework in his classes)
- (2) The military commander ***did away with*** the traitor.
(Meaning: had him killed for being a traitor)

Do over *(separable):* 1. Do again, to repeat something, as in this example: *If the teacher did not approve the project, the student was allowed to **do** it **over**.*

More examples:
- (1) The owner didn't like the paint job on his house and asked the painter to ***do*** it ***over***.
- (1) As the golfer swung the club someone in the crowd made a loud noise. The golfer was allowed to ***do*** that shot ***over***.

Do without *(inseparable):* 1. To be deprived of; to continue living minus some of the things you have been used to in your life in the past, as in this example: *When I was young, we had to **do without** nice clothes and fine food because we had very little money.*

More examples:
- (1) The water heater stopped working so we will have to ***do without*** hot water tonight.
- (1) The survivors of the shipwreck had to ***do without*** clean water for many days.

Dress up (separable): 1. To put nice clothes on, as in this example: *My wife and I **dressed up** and went to a nice restaurant for dinner.* 2. To fix something up to look better, as in this example: *The company **dressed up** its headquarters to make a better impression on visitors.* (Meaning: The company improved the looks of the building where their main headquarters was located so that visitors would be impressed.)

   More examples:
- (1) Tonight is the night that we are going to the big dance. We are going to have to ***dress up*** tonight.
- (2) The chef will often ***dress up*** his dishes (meals) to look more delicious. (Meaning: the chef will arrange the food on the plate to look more appealing.)

Drink down (separable): 1. Drink all of something, usually in one pass, as in this example: *The marathon runners stopped at the water table, **drank down** the water, and continued running.*

   More examples:
- (1) During a beer-drinking contest, the competitors will ***drink down*** their mug of beer.
- (1) The medicine doesn't taste good so you will have to ***drink*** it ***down*** quickly.

Drink up (separable): 1. Finish drinking something, as in this example: *We were so thirsty that we **drank up** all of the ice tea in the refrigerator.* 2. To take in, to absorb, as in this example: *We took the dog out to play with a ball. When he came back to the house, he **drank up** all of his water in his water bowl.*

More examples:
- (1) I told my children to *__drink up__* their milk so we could leave for the beach.
- (2) The ground was so dry that it *__drank up__* the moisture from the new rain.

__Drop in__ (inseparable): 1. To visit unexpectedly or with little warning, as in this example: *After work, I __dropped in__ at the library and got a book.*
More examples:
- (1) On the way home, we decided to *__drop in__* on our friends.
- (1) It is usually not polite to *__drop in__* on someone unless they are a relative or a very close friend.

__Drop off__ (separable): 1. To leave something somewhere without spending much time at the location; to stop somewhere unexpectedly and leave something, as in this example: *On the way home from school I __dropped__ my laundry __off__ at the cleaners.*
More examples:
- (1) On the way to work I *__dropped__* my daughter *__off__* at school.
- (1) The postman *__dropped off__* a package at our house.

__Drop out__ (inseparable): 1. To stop participating in something; to quit, as in this example: *The student __dropped out__ of the advanced class because it was too difficult for him.* 2. To stop doing what everyone else is doing; to ignore the rules of normal society and live a life based on your own ideas, as in this example: *The hippies **dropped out** in the 1960s and 1970s because they didn't trust the ways of normal society.*

More examples:
- (1) The runner ***dropped out*** of the race in exhaustion.
- (2) Marco decided to ***drop out*** and sail around the world on his own sailboat.

Dry off *(separable):* 1. To remove water or moisture from someone or something, as in this example: *I **dried off** the table with a towel.*

More examples:
- (1) After we got out of the swimming pool we ***dried*** ourselves ***off***.
- (1) My cell phone fell in the water so dried it off and took the battery out.

Dry out *(separable):* 1. All moisture evaporating out of something over time; all the moistness leaves something, as in this example: *I stepped in some water during the rainstorm. When I returned home I **dried out** my shoes with the help of a hair dryer.*

More examples:
- (1) Rain came in the window and got the rug wet. It took two weeks to ***dry*** the rug ***out***.
- (1) Sometimes the skin can ***dry out*** during the winter season. Some women put skin moisturizer on themselves to prevent their skin from ***drying out***.

Dry up *(separable):* 1. When moisture leaves something because of evaporation, as in this example: *The sun came out* *and the ground **dried up**.* 2. When the amount of something gets smaller and disappears, as in this example: *Our supply of corn chips has **dried up**. Would someone go to the food store and get some more.*

More examples:
- ❑ (1) The towel that was wet yesterday has ***dried up*** over night.
- ❑ (2) Our coffee supply has ***dried up***, someone better go to the store and get some more coffee.

Eat up *(separable):* 1. To eat all of something, as in this example: *I **ate up** all of the cake in the refrigerator. My roommates were really mad.* 2. To use resources usually at a high rate of speed, as in this example: *Shopping at that expensive store really **eats up** my bank account.* 3. *(slang)* To really enjoy or embrace something, as in this example: *The political candidate told the people they wouldn't have to pay taxes if they elect him. The people were **eating** it **up**.*

More examples:
- ❑ (1) The sushi was great. We ***ate*** it all ***up***. (English speakers use "all" to mean "completely.")
- ❑ (2) That car really ***eats up*** gas.
- ❑ (3) When we were doing our song on stage the audience was really ***eating*** it ***up***. (Meaning: the audience really liked our song)

Eat out *(inseparable):* 1. To eat at a location away from home, at a restaurant or elsewhere, as in this example: *We **ate out** at the club last night.*

More examples:
- (1) We *ate out* last night. I really liked that restaurant.
- (1) I'm tired of cooking, let's *eat out*.

Empty out (separable): 1. Completely removing the contents of something, as in this example: *I emptied out my closet trying to find my ice skates.*
More examples:
- (1) We *emptied out* the refrigerator so that we could clean it.
- (1) The woman *emptied out* her purse looking for her drivers license.

End up (inseparable): 1. To finish with a result; resulting in, as in this example: *Sabine ended up going to university in Cologne.*
More examples:
- (1) We *ended up* going to California for our vacation because we didn't have enough money to go to Paris.
- (1) The school *ended up* closing because it didn't have enough money to pay the teachers.

Fall apart (inseparable): 1. To break down, collapse, as in this example: *The old building was falling apart because of lack of care.* 2. To become emotionally unstable or weak, usually due to some situation or circumstance, as in this example: *The woman fell apart and started to cry when she talked about her mother.*
More examples:
- (1) The old chair *fell apart* when Jason tried to sit in it.

- (2) My colleague *fell apart* when he was told that he would be laid off in two months.

Fall behind (inseparable): 1. To fail to keep up a pace, to lag behind, as in this example: *The student fell behind the rest of the class because he was always absent.*
   More examples:
   - (1) The tired runner *fell behind* the rest of the runners.
   - (1) We *fell behind* in our car payments and the bank was angry. (Meaning: we could not continue to make payments when the bank required.)

Fall down (inseparable): 1. To drop or come down from a higher position, usually to the ground, as in this example: *The runner fell down during the marathon competition.* 2. Fail to meet expectations, as in this example: *The company fell down on its obligation to complete the production of its product.*
   More examples:
   - (1) Gina *fell down* and hurt her knee while trying to learn how to ice skate.
   - (2) Jim's boss was really mad with him because he *fell down* on the job that he was given. (Meaning: Jim did not do his job right and because of this his boss was mad at him.)

Fall for (inseparable): 1. To believe something that was not true and sometimes act on that belief; to be deceived or swindled, as in this example: *I can't believe I fell for that advertisement.* The advertisement said that I would get a free car if I bought one of

their products. 2. To feel love for, as in this example: *I really fell for the girl with the red hair.*
>   **More examples:**
>   - (1) My friend *fell for* that work-at-home advertisement on the Internet and lost $100.
>   - (2) The first time I saw my wife I *fell for* her immediately.

Fall off (inseparable): 1. To become less, decrease, as in this example: *Our store sales fell off by 50% last week. We have to advertise more.* 2. To drop from a higher level to a lower place, usually the thing or person was perched on something above the ground, like a chair or the branch of a tree, etc., as in this example: *The book fell off the table and onto the floor.*
>   **More examples:**
>   - (1) The boy *fell off* the chair.
>   - (2) Stock prices *fell off* sharply. (Meaning: stock prices went down rapidly.)

Fall out (inseparable): 1. To leave a military formation, as in this example: *After the military exercise was finished, the commander asked the men to fall out and go have dinner.* 2. To quarrel, as in this example: *The shopkeeper and the customer fell out over the price of bread.* 3. To fall or drop from something you were in, like a chair, car or plane, and fall to the ground or a lower elevation, as in this example: *I fell out of my chair when I heard that my daughter was getting married.* (Note: sometimes this phrasal verb is used in a light, playful way, meaning that a person was surprised about something).

More examples:
- (1) The captain ordered his men to *fall out* and go back to their barracks.
- (2) The two women *fell out* over the same man.
- (3) The man was laughing so hard he *fell out* of his chair.

Fall over (inseparable): 1. To tumble or drop from a higher place to a lower one with the help of gravity and sometimes because of an obstacle (the feeling of "fall over" is that there is usually motion, movement or some causative element first and then, unexpectedly, someone or something tumbles to the ground or down with the help of gravity, sometimes because of an obstacle in their path), as in this example: *The flower pot fell over and broke.* 2. To *fall over* oneself means to make a lot of effort to help someone out (the feeling of this phrase is that someone really wants to please someone else by showing them how much they want to help or accomplish something for them), as in this example: *The student fell over himself trying to make a good impression on the rest of the class.*

More examples:
- (1) The children ran into the table and the lamp *fell over* and broke.
- (2) The new employee *fell over* herself trying to please her boss.

Fall through (inseparable): 1. To drop down into an opening and continue to the ground or lower location, as in this example: *The workman **fell through** a hole in the roof.* 2. When something fails or is not completed, as in this example: *The business deal between the two companies **fell through**.*

More examples:
- (1) The sailor **fell through** the open hatch and had to be taken to the hospital.
- (2) We were going to go to Japan for our vacation but those plans **fell through** and we decided to go somewhere else.

Feel up to (inseparable): 1. To be in the mood, to have the energy, to be healthy/well enough to do something (a variation of this phrase with the same meaning is *to be up to*), as in this example: *I didn't **feel up to** going to work today so I stayed home.*

More examples:
- (1) I told my friends that I wasn't **feeling up to** playing soccer this afternoon. They would have to find someone else for their team.
- (1) We were excited about going snowboarding. We were **feeling up to** trying some new techniques.

Fight back (inseparable): 1. To defend oneself in a conflict. (You get the feeling from this phrase that someone really wants to fight back because they were attacked), as in this

example: *Our soccer team was losing 1-0. We decided to **fight back** because we wanted to win.*
   More examples:
   - (1) Our football team was losing 3 to 1 and we really wanted to ***fight back*** and win.
   - (1) The woman ***fought back*** against her attacker and then ran away.

Figure on *(inseparable):* 1. To plan on, as in this example: *We **figure on** completing our English studies by next June.*
   More examples:
   - (1) We had to cut our vacation short because we didn't ***figure on*** the high cost of hotel accommodations.
   - (1) You should ***figure on*** spending at least two hours at the airport for checking in and security checks.

Figure out *(separable):* 1. To uncover the answer, to think something through and come up with the answer, as in this example: *I **figured out** why we cannot get a visa to enter that country. They just changed governments.*
   More examples:
   - (1) We couldn't ***figure out*** the math problem.
   - (1) I couldn't ***figure out*** why my mother was so mad at me.

Fill in *(separable):* 1. To give information, usually the information is new, as in this example: *I was absent from work for two weeks. My colleague **filled** me **in** on what happened in the office while I was gone.* 2. To substitute, as in this example:

Nancy Yee filled in for her colleague, Wendy, while Wendy was in Europe. 3. To put something like dirt or water into a void or hole to build up to an even level, as in this example: *After putting the fuel tank in the ground, the company **filled in** the hole.*

More examples:
- (1) My classmate *filled* me *in* on what homework was due today. (Meaning: One classmate told the other classmate about the homework assignment due today.)
- (2) Janice stayed home sick so Yuki *filled in* for her. (Yuki substituted for Janice because Janice was sick.)
- (3) The workers shoveled dirt into the hole to *fill* it *in*. (Meaning: the workers put dirt back into the hole.)

Fill out *(separable):* 1. To complete, as in this example: *The school secretary asked me to **fill out** the form.* 2. To gain weight, as in this example: *I stopped exercising three months ago and now I'm starting to **fill out**.*

More examples:
- (1) The custom's official asked me to *fill out* the form.
- (2) My friend Paco really *filled out*. (Meaning: Paco gained weight.)

Fill up *(separable):* 1.To put liquid or other substance into a container to replenish supply, as in this example: *I **filled up** the ice tea pitcher and put it in the refrigerator.* 2. Can refer to eating enough food, as in this example: *I **filled up** on salad and didn't feel like eating anything else.* 3. Can refer to a room or building being crowded with people, as in this example: *The room **filled***

up to capacity. (Meaning: The room was full of people. The number of people legally allowed in the room, or the comfort of the people already in the room, would determine if it was filled up.)
> **More examples:**
> - (1) Erika went to the gas station to ***fill*** her car ***up*** with gas. (Note: Americans say, "fill the car up with gas" when they mean fill the gas tank of the car up with gas.")
> - (2) The father told his daughter not to ***fill up*** on chocolate because they were going to have dinner in one hour.
> - (3) It was a great celebration. There were so many people at the party that the room was ***filled up***.

Find out (separable): 1. To discover, to learn of, as in this example: *We just **found out** that our flight was cancelled.*
> **More examples:**
> - (1) His classmates ***found out*** that his birthday was next week and they decided to have a party for him.
> - (1) The police ***found out*** that the thief was hiding in the building.

Fix up (separable): 1. To renovate, to put in good condition, as in this example: *They **fixed up** the meeting room. They painted it and bought new furniture.*
> **More examples:**
> - (1) When they finished ***fixing up*** the old car it looked like new.

- (1) The old house looked terrible before they _fixed_ it _up_.

Flip out (inseparable): 1. To get angry or very anxious, as in this example: *He really **flipped out** when he saw his electric bill.* 2. To become emotional, as in this example: *Rita **flipped out** when they told her she won the lottery.*

More examples:
- (1) My mother _flipped out_ when she found out I spent the money on a new dress. I was supposed to buy groceries with that money.
- (2) The student _flipped out_ when she got her exam back with a perfect score.

Float around (separable): 1. When something or someone moves through space as if they were supported by liquid or air, moving from one location to another with no real focus, as in this example: *The leaves were **floating around** in the swimming pool.*

More examples:
- (1) The hostess of the party was _floating around_ talking to this couple and then that couple.
- (1) The toy sailboat was _floating around_ in the bath tube.

Follow through (inseparable): 1. To complete an action or responsibility, as in this example: *The four of us were able to **follow through** with our promise to travel around the world in eight months.* 2. In sports to continue a movement after contact, for example, _follow through_ with a golf swing, as in this example:

When you kick a soccer ball you have to <u>follow through</u> the ball with your foot.

More examples:
- (1) Our project failed because we didn't <u>follow through</u> and complete the work that was necessary.
- (2) After Martina hits the tennis ball she <u>follows through</u>.

Follow up (separable): 1. When someone makes an additional effort to check on or complete something that he or she was interested in, or interested in doing (this phrase is usually used to talk about someone continuing to do something or research something for the purpose of solving a problem, getting a job done, or learning more about something), as in this example: *Jack did some research about the company on the Internet and then <u>followed</u> that <u>up</u> with a phone call to the company.*

More examples:
- (1) Hiro called the cell phone company to find out if they had the model and color cell phone that he wanted. A salesman at the company <u>followed up</u> on Hiro's request and called him back to tell him they did have the model and color he wanted.
- (2) The police <u>followed up</u> on a tip that the Main Street bank was going to be robbed at 5pm. When the robbers came, the police were waiting for them.

Fool around (inseparable): 1. Usually someone not taking something seriously, as in this example: *We will never get our* *work done because we are **fooling around** too much.* 2. Can mean that a girlfriend or boyfriend, husband or wife, is cheating on the other, as in this example: *Hilde's boyfriend caught her **fooling around** with another man and told her he didn't want to see her again.*

> **More examples:**
> - (1) The students ***fooled around*** the whole day and didn't learn anything.
> - (2) The wife found out that her husband had been ***fooling around*** with another woman.

Freak out *(inseparable):* 1. *(informal)* Becoming emotionally unstable because of something that happened (Note: Americans can use this phrasal verb in a playful way, not meaning it in a serious way), as in this example: *I **freaked out** when my friend told me that the cute boy in our class was interested in me.*

> **More examples:**
> - (1) My mother ***freaked out*** when I brought the lizard home.
> - (1) Billy wore the Halloween mask to school to ***freak out*** his classmates.

Chapter 3 review

*Phrasal verbs beginning with the letters **D, E, and F***

*Instructions: read and /or listen carefully to the sentences below. Fill in the blank spaces with the correct **preposition, particle,** or **adverb**. The answers can be found in this chapter (above).*

1. The newspaper article deals _____ the problem of drugs in big cities.

2. The wife found out that her husband had been fooling _____ with another woman.

3. After Martina hits the tennis ball she follows _____.

4. The toy sailboat was floating _____ in the bath tube.

5. The police found _____ that the thief was hiding in the building.

6. The old house looked terrible before they fixed it _____.

7. The student flipped _____ when she got her exam back with a perfect score.

8. The custom's official asked me to fill _____ the form.

9. We had to cut our vacation short because we didn't figure ___ the high cost of hotel accommodations.

10. The woman fought _____ against her attacker and then ran away.

11. The new employee fell _____ herself trying to please her boss.

Page 59

12. The sailor fell _____ the open hatch and had to be taken to the hospital.

13. The boy fell _____ the chair.

14. Gina fell _____ and hurt her knee while trying to learn how to ice skate.

15. The school ended ____ closing because it didn't have enough money to pay the teachers.

16. We emptied _____ the refrigerator so that we could clean it.

17. That American car really eats ____ gas.

18. The towel that was wet yesterday has dried ___ over night.

19. The runner dropped _____ of the race in exhaustion.

20. On the way to work I dropped my daughter _____ at school.

Chapter 4

*Phrasal verbs beginning with the letter **G***

Read and / or listen to each of these phrasal verbs beginning with the letter G, followed by their meanings and then some examples of how they are used in real English sentences.

There are two kinds of phrasal verbs, separable and inseparable. Separable phrasal verbs can take an object between the verb and the preposition. For example: *My father **picked** me **up** after school and drove me home.* Inseparable phrasal verbs cannot take an object between the verb and the preposition. For example: *I asked my friends to **come along** with me to the Christmas party.* ***Come along*** cannot be separated by an object.

The numbers in front of the examples that are in parenthesis (), correspond the to number of the explanation found directly above. So, for example: 1. *explanation* . . . refers to (1) *example* . . . . If there is only one explanation or meaning given for the phrasal verb, then there will be two examples given for the one explanation. Both examples will be marked with (1).

If you have the accompanying Focus on English mp3 audio book (available separately from the school store or from www.FOEBooks.com) listen to each of the phrasal verbs, followed by their meanings and then some examples of how they are used in real English sentences. Each example will be spoken twice. There will be a review at the end of this chapter.

Page 61

There will be a review at the end of this chapter.

Phrasal verbs beginning with the letter G

Get ahead (inseparable): 1. To improve your position or situation; to make progress, as in this example: *The man worked at two jobs to try to **get ahead** and improve his monthly income.*
More examples:
- (1) It is difficult to **get ahead** if you don't work hard.
- (1) After I got a raise at work I was able to **get ahead** and pay all of my bills.

Get along (inseparable): 1. Usually refers to humans or animals and means to coexist harmoniously, as in this example: *The coworkers liked each other and got along very well.* 2. Can also mean to get older, as in this example: *My grandfather is getting along in years and has to be helped when he enters or leaves a car.* 3. Sometimes refers to economics with the following meaning: a person or group is able to exist without undue hardship, as in this example: *I don't make much money as work, but I get along okay.*
More examples:
- (1) We have a dog and a cat and they **get along** just fine.
- (2) We all **get along** in years as time goes by.
- (3) The couple living in the old house is able to get along on their pension checks.

Page 62

Get around to *(inseparable):* 1. To do something whenever the person is in the mood, or has time to do it. The feeling of this usage is that the person or group is lazy or very busy and will not do something until the time is right or until they feel like it, as in this example: *The road out in front of our house needs urgent repair, but the Roads Department said that they are not in a hurry and will fix the road when they **get around to** it.*

More examples:
- (1) My daughter thinks that she should do her chores when she gets around to it.
- (1) I'll do my homework when I get around to it.

Get away *(inseparable and separable depending on the content of the sentence):* 1. To leave to go on vacation (the feeling of this expression is that you need a rest or a real change and you are leaving everything behind for a little while and going on vacation), as in this example: *I've had enough of work; I need to **get away** for a short vacation;* 2. To get away ***with*** something is when no one detects or catches or cares about something that was done that was sneaky or not the usually accepted way of doing something, as in this example: *Tom **got away** with not doing his homework because the teacher did not check homework today.* 3. *(separable)* To separate something or someone from something or someone, as in this example: *I hate snakes, **get** that snake **away** from me!*

More examples:
- (1) It is nice to leave the city for a while and ***get away*** to the country.

- (2) The clerk ***got away*** with not giving the customer the correct change.
- (3) ***Get*** that cat ***away*** from me; I am allergic to cat hair!

Get back *(inseparable and separable depending on the content of the sentence):* 1. Usually a command that means to keep a distance from something or someone usually because there is danger, as in this example: ***Get back****! It is dangerous to enter this area*; 2. To return to where one was before, as in this example: *The party lasted almost all night and I didn't **get back** home until 5am*; 3. To have something returned that one once owned or possessed before, as in this example: *I **got** my exam paper **back** from the teacher yesterday. I got an A on the exam.*

More examples:
- (1) ***Get back****,* the building may collapse any time!
- (2) When I ***got back*** to my home country, my family was waiting for me.
- (3) The thief took my purse, but I ***got*** my wallet ***back*** when the police found it in the trash.

Get back at *(inseparable):* 1. To retaliate against., as in this example: *The soccer team from Newbury beat us last week, but this week we **got back at** them with a 4-2 win.*

More examples:
- (1) The little girl was mad at her mom, so she ***got back at*** her by not cleaning her room.
- (1) If you complain to the government, the government may ***get back at*** you by increasing your taxes.

Get back to *(inseparable):* 1. To return to some place or something that was being said or done, as in this example: *I like talking about this subject, but I would like to **get back to** the subject that we were talking about in the beginning.*
- More examples:
  - ❑ (1) To ***get back to*** our hotel we had to take a taxi.
  - ❑ (1) We should not have gone on a long hike because now we won't ***get back to*** the camp for at least four hours.

Get behind *(inseparable):* 1. To support; to give support to something or someone, as in this example: *We really **got behind** our time during the game.* 2. To position oneself or something to the rear of something or someone; frequently used as a command to emphasize urgency or danger, as in this example: *If you **get behind** me you will be safe from harm.*
- More examples:
  - ❑ (1) Cancer research is important so my family ***got behind*** the Cancer Society when they asked for volunteers.
  - ❑ (2) The soldiers ***got behind*** the wall to protect themselves from the enemy bullets.

Get by *(inseparable):* 1. When someone or a group is able to survive (but not much more) by their efforts, or create barely acceptable action results, as in this example: *While we were lost in the woods we **got by** on berries and whatever we could find to eat.* 2. To move around or by someone or something on the way to a destination beyond, as in this example: *May I **get by** you? I want to sit in the front row.*
- More examples:

- ❑ (1) The survivors ***got by*** on very little food and water.
- ❑ (2) The soccer play ran down the field, ***got by*** one player and kicked the ball towards the goal.

Get down *(inseparable and separable depending on the content of the sentence):* 1. To climb or move downward or from a higher place to a lower place, as in this example: *The workers **got down** off of the roof and went home.* 2. (separable) To make feel melancholy or depressed, as in this example: *I got a poor grade on the exam, but I didn't let that **get** me **down**.*

More examples:
- ❑ (1) The cat ***got down*** off the table and ate dinner.
- ❑ (2) The boxer hated to lose. Losing really ***gets*** him ***down***.

Get in (into) *(inseparable and separable depending on the content of the sentence):* 1. To climb into or enter usually an enclosed area of some kind like a building or a car, as in this example: *I **got in** (or into) the taxi and asked the driver to take me to River Street.* 2. To fit something or someone in or into something, as in this example: *We couldn't **get** all of the milk **in** (or into) the jar.* 3. To arrive, as in this example: *After the long drive, we **got in** at 2am;* 4. To find time for something, an event or activity, as in this example: *We were able to **get in** some tennis during our business trip to Spain.*

More examples:
- ❑ (1) We all ***got in*** the bus and began singing.
- ❑ (2) I really gained weight; I couldn't ***get into*** that size 9 dress.

- (3) The train *got in* at 4:56pm, almost 1 hour late!
- (4) We were supposed to be working, but we *got* some shopping *in* during the day.

Get off (inseparable and separable depending on the content of the sentence): 1. To disembark, as in this example: *When we reached Frankfurt, everyone **got off** the train.* 2. Used in expressing the time when you stop doing something, like working, as in this example: *We **got off** work at 5pm.* 3. When someone stops talking on the phone and hangs up, as in this example: *My daughter was on the phone for about an hour. She finally **got off** at 8:30pm.* 4. Used to express difficulty in removing something, as in this example: *I can't **get** this stain **off** of my blouse.*

More examples:
- (1) Driver, I would like to *get off* at 23rd Street.
- (2) We're going to the movies tonight, what time do you *get off* school? Maybe you can go with us.
- (3) As soon as my wife *gets off* the phone I will call the doctor and make an appointment to see him.
- (4) I took the pants to the cleaner to see if they could *get* the black mark *off* of my pants.

Get off on (slang) (inseparable): 1. Used to express one's pleasure at doing something, as in this example: *I really **get off on** walking in nature.*

More examples:
- (1) I really *get off on* doing math.

- (1) This is the third time we've seen that movie; *we* really *get off on* it.

Get on (inseparable): 1. To board transportation, as in this example: *We **got on** the bus and went to the city center.* 2. To move towards and then sit, stand or recline on something, as in this example: *When the actress **got on** the stage she sang a love song.* 3. To take action to do something or continue doing something (common British usage), as in this example: *It is important to **get on** with taking the exam because you only have five minutes left.*

More examples:
- (1) We *got on* the plane and 2pm and flew to Tokyo.
- (2) She *got on* the table and started dancing.
- (3) Let's *get on* with finishing this project so that we can go home.

Get out (inseparable or separable depending on usage): 1. Used to express leaving or disembarking, as in this example: *We **got out** of the taxi and went into the restaurant.* 2. Used to express the feeling of rescue or helping to leave or escape someplace, as in this example: *There was a practice fire drill in our building and we had to **get out** of the building as quickly as possible.* 3. Used to have the same meaning as get away, to take a rest, vacation or break and go somewhere that is different than where you usually are as in this example: *We have been working too hard. We need to **get out** and enjoy ourselves more.* 4. To make known, to make information widely available, information that was usually private, kept secret, or not generally known, as in this

example: *When the news **got out** about Paul and Debbie's wedding, everyone was very surprised.*
More examples:
- (1) We told the Taxi drive to stop on Broadway. Then we ***got out*** of the taxi and went to a theater.
- (2) When the earthquake came we ***got out*** of the building quickly.
- (3) We ***got out*** of the city for a while to enjoy ourselves in the country.
- (4) When the news about John getting fired ***got out***, we were all shocked.

Get out of *(inseparable or separable depending on usage):* 1. (inseparable) To remove oneself from something or some obligation, as in this example: *The student **got out of** having to take the exam because he already had a high mark in that class.* 2. (inseparable) Used to express the idea of reward for doing something, as in this example: *This is what we **get out of** working for that company: a high salary and good benefits.* 3. (separable) Used to express the idea of forcibly getting something from someone or something, as in this example: *She **got** the information she needed **out of** the old woman by threatening her.*
More examples:
- (1) I ***got out of*** having to go to the meeting because I had a dental appointment at that time.
- (2) He didn't sell his house because he couldn't ***get*** enough money ***out of*** it.
- (3) The police ***got*** the information about the robbery ***out of*** the witness.

Get over (inseparable): 1. To recover, as in this example: *I just got over the flu.* 2. Used in commands or to express urgency when you want someone to come to where you are located, as in this example: *Get over here, I want to show you something interesting in the water!*

More examples:
- (1) Miho was hospitalized for an infection; I hope she *gets over* it soon.
- (2) You'd better *get over* to the office, the director wants to talk to you.

Get over with (separable): 1. Used when you want to express wanting to complete something or finish something, as in this example: *Boy, I'm worried about this exam. I can't wait to get it over with.*

More examples:
- (1) I have to go to the dentist tomorrow. I hate going to the dentist. I want to *get* it *over with* as soon as possible.
- (1) That medicine tastes terrible, so I'd better drink it fast and *get* it *over with*.

Get through (inseparable): 1. Used to express struggling to finish something, as in this example: *This has been a bad day, I will be glad when I get through it.* 2. Used to express the need to communicate something to someone, or communication with someone, as in this example: *The teacher got through to us that we needed to study for the difficult exam.*

More examples:
- (1) Try to *get through* the first part of the exam as quickly as possible, because you only have one hour to finish.
- (2) The parents tried to *get through* to their daughter that it was dangerous to walk home alone in the dark.

Get to (inseparable): 1. To arrive at or reach a place, idea or situation, as in this example: *Excuse me, how do we **get to** the center of town?* 2. Used to express time when one is talking about starting to do something, as in this example: *I am really busy now, I will cut the grass when I **get to** it.*

More examples:
- (1) The men looked at the map to decide how to *get to* the top of the mountain.
- (2) I have about ten things to do right now, I will *get to* that project in about an hour.

Get together (separable): 1. To meet and spend time with, as in this example: *The family **got together** for Christmas.* 2. To become organized for the purpose of accomplishing a task or action, as in this example: *We **got** the papers **together** so that we could meet with the company representative.* 3. To focus or bring your emotions together so that you are calm and rational, as in this example: *Before taking a big exam, I am always very nervous. My solution to this is to spend a couple of minutes relaxing and **getting** it **together** so that I am calm and can think clearly.*

More examples:
- (1) The students *got together* and had a party.

- (2) We have to *get* our plan *together* so that we can defeat the other team.
- (3) After about two hours of crying, my sister finally *got* it *together*, had a cup of tea, and calmed down.

Get up (inseparable): 1. To awaken, as in this example: *I got up at 6:30am and went for a walk.* 2. To raise, for example, money or resources, as in this example: *Our organization had to get up enough money to help the poor in our town.* 3. To rise up from a lower position, as in this example: *I got up and turned off the TV.*

More examples:
- (1) We all had to *get up* at 8 o'clock to go to breakfast.
- (2) Our group had to *get up* enough money to pay for the tickets.
- (3) She *got up* and left the room.

Give away (separable): 1. To make a gift of, as in this example: *The company gave away free samples of their product.* 2. To present a bride to the groom at a wedding ceremony (The father is the presenter in American custom), as in this example: *The father gave the bride away at the alter of the church.* 3. To reveal or make known, often accidentally, as in this example: *She drank too much at the party and gave away our secret.* 4. To betray, as in this example: *The captured soldier gave away our hiding place to the enemy* (Meaning: the captured soldier, under pressure, told the enemy where we were hiding).

More examples:

- (1) We *gave away* Christmas presents to the poor children.
- (2) Her father *gave* her *away* on her wedding day.
- (3) While speaking to her boss, I accidentally *gave away* the real reason why my friend was absent from work yesterday.
- (4) Our loud talking *gave away* our location in the building.

Give back (separable): 1. To return, as in this example: *I gave the tools back to my friend.*
More examples:
- (1) I borrowed a bicycle from my friend and, two days later, I *gave* it *back*.
- (2) After the purchase, the shopkeeper *gave* me $1.10 *back* as change.

Give in (inseparable): 1. To relent, to cease opposition to, to yield, as in this example: *After arguing for two hours, I finally gave in.* 2. To submit or hand in, as in this example: *The students gave in their homework.*
More examples:
- (1) My friend asked me to lend her money and after three hours I finally *gave in* and lent her $10.
- (2) Everyone had to *give in* his or her exam after one hour.

Give out (separable): 1. To run out of energy or to fail while proceeding with some action, as in this example: *The car finally gave out* after four hours of trying to climb the mountain. 2. To distribute something, as in this example: *The teacher gave out the exams.* 3. To emit as a noise, as in this example: *The alarm clock gave out a loud ringing noise.*

More examples:
- (1) I *gave out* after two hours of running.
- (2) My boss *gave out* our paychecks.
- (3) The gun *gave out* a loud bang!

Give up (separable): 1. To surrender; to admit defeat, as in this example: *The enemy soldiers gave up after a long fight.* 2. To stop doing or performing an action, as in this example: *The wolf gave up chasing the rabbit.* 3. To part with something or someone, as in this example: *The family had to give up everything to leave their country and move to Europe.* 4. To express losing hope or opportunity, as in this example: *I give up, I will never understand math!* 5. To abandon doing something, or abandon the idea of doing something, as in this example: *We gave up the idea of hiking to the top of the mountain.*

More examples:
- (1) The police chased the thief until he *gave up*.
- (2) After two hours, I *gave up* riding my bike in the rain.
- (3) I went on a diet; I had to *give up* eating candy.
- (4) After two days without food or water, the survivors almost *gave up* hope.
- (5) We *gave up* the idea of going to Asia.

Go about (inseparable):   1.   To do or to undertake a responsibility, action or project; this phrase also has the feeling of 'continuing' an action as usual, as in this example: *After the meeting, we went back to our offices and **went about** our usual business.*

> **More examples:**
> - (1) We ignored all of the noise outside and **went about** our business.
> - (2) We didn't get upset by the small earthquake and **went about** our business after the shaking stopped.

Go after (inseparable):   1.   To pursue or chase, as in this example: *The police **went after** the escaped prisoner.* 2. Try to get or obtain something, for example, like a sales goal, university degree, or English proficiency, as in this example: *After high school, I **went after** my degree in economics at the University of Hawaii.*

> **More examples:**
> - (1) During the game, two of our players **went after** their star player to try to stop the goal.
> - (2) After attending university, I **went after** a career in teaching.

Go ahead (inseparable): 1. Proceed forward or move forward or take action, as in this example: *We decided to **go ahead** with the project.* 2. Permission to do something, as in this example: *My daughter asked me if she could play with her friends and I told her to **go ahead** but come home in about two hours.*

> **More examples:**

Page 75

- (1) We *went ahead* with the competition even though it was raining.
- (2) Mom, can I go to the movies?
  Go ahead, but be home by 10pm.

Go along with (inseparable): 1. To agree with, as in this example: *My boss went along with my idea.* 2. To accompany, as in this example: *We went along with the tour group to see the ancient ruins.*

More examples:
- (1) We *went along* with the committee's decision.
- (1) Stefan *went along* with his friend to the pizza parlor for lunch.

Go around (inseparable): 1. To go here and there, move from place to place, as in this example: *We went around the mall looking at different things.* 2. To avoid something by moving in a curve pattern, as in this example: *We went around the obstacle in the road.* 3. To spin, as in this example: *We almost got sick on the amusement park ride because it went around very fast.* 4. To be in plain sight of other people while in a certain condition or situation, as in this example: *I went around with the ketchup stain on my shirt all day. I was so embarrassed.* 5. Something being distributed or communicated, as in this example: *The bad news about the economy went around very quickly.*

More examples:
- (1) We spend the day *going around* the city, first to the different historic buildings, and then to the different stores.

- (2) On our way to lunch, my colleagues and I found a way to quickly *get around* the construction blockades in the middle of the walkway.
- (3) The wheels of the machinery *went around* very quickly.
- (4) Marco *went around* all day with two different colored socks on.
- (5) When Shino quit the company, the news *got around* quickly.

Go away (inseparable): 1. To leave, to take leave of, as in this example: *We went away for the holiday.* 2. Also used to express ceasing or stopping an annoyance as in this example: *I wish this noise would go away.*

More examples:
- (1) When I asked where Kazu was, his colleagues told me that he *went away* to New York.
- (2) The smell coming from the other room was terrible, we hoped it would *go away*.

Go back (inseparable): 1. To return to (this can refer to physically returning to a place, as in this example: *We liked Los Vegas so much we went back again.* 2. Can refer to returning in one's mind to a time, as in this example: *In our minds, we went back to the time when we were in high school.* 3. (*go back on*) to renege, especially relating to promises or agreements, as in this example: *The politician went back on his word that he would help everyone get health insurance.*

More examples:

- (1) We *went back* to our office after lunch.
- (2) The history book talked about things that happened in the past: it *went back* to the Roman times.
- (3) She left her boyfriend because he *went back on* his word that he would marry her.

Go beyond (inseparable): 1. To do more than the required amount; to exceed the intended goal or to do more than was expected, as in this example: *The way to succeed in business is to go beyond your customers' expectations.* 2. To go further than a physical location, as in this example: *Go beyond the water fountain and the English classroom is on your right.*

More examples:
- (1) She *went beyond* her boss' expectations when she folded all of the letters and put them into envelopes.
- (2) *Go* three stores *beyond* the restaurant and you will find the bookstore.

Go by (inseparable): 1. To pass usually close to you or a group; or elapse (as with time), as in this example: *Sometimes it seems that time goes by very quickly; In Rome, we passed by a group of tourists who were looking at the coliseum.* 2. Similar to drop by, meaning to stop for a short visit, as in this example: *Let's go by my sister's house for a little visit.*

More examples:
- (1) In the town center, we *went by* a group of political demonstrators.

- (1) When you are taking an exam, time seems to *go by* too quickly.
- (2) On the way to town, we *went by* an Italian restaurant to look at the menu.

Go down (inseparable): 1. Referring to something dropping below the horizon, as in this example: *The sun went down and it was a beautiful evening.* 2. To go to a lower position or location, as in this example: *The wine maker went down into the cellar to get some wine.* 3. When a computer, computer network or machinery stops working, as in this example: *I'm sorry but I cannot get your information right now because my computer went down.* 4. Referring to swallowing something, as in this example: *The cough medicine went down easy.*

More examples:
- (1) The moon *went down* over the horizon and the sun started to come up.
- (2) The secretary *went down* to the second floor to get the papers.
- (3) The electrical generator *went down* and the town didn't have electricity.
- (4) If you take this medicine with a little honey, it will *go down* easily.

Go for (inseparable): 1. To attack, as in this example: *The dog went for the child and bit her on the leg.* 2. To have a special liking for something or someone, as in this example: *When I first met my wife I really went for her.* 3. To make an attempt to achieve or get something, as in this example: *The student studied*

hard for the exam because he wanted to *go for* the highest possible mark. 4. Used to express equality, for example: *What goes for me goes for you (meaning, rules apply equally to me and to you).*
More examples:
- (1) The opponents *went for* each other.
- (2) She *really goes* for chocolate.
- (3) The runner *went for* first place in the competition.
- (4) What *goes for* one employee should *go for* all employees.

Go in (inseparable): 1. To enter into something, usually an enclosed area, as in this example: *We went in(to) the dark room.* 2. Used to mean that something belongs in a certain place, as in this example: *The book goes in the drawer.* 3. Used to mean **to advance into an area** for the purpose of defeating an enemy or stopping a riot, as in this example: *The police went into the riot area to stop the destruction.* 4. Go in *for* is used to show preference for something, for example: *I don't go in for tennis.*
More examples:
- (1) The tour group *went in*(to) the cathedral.
- (2) The pencils *go in* the drawer.
- (3) The soldiers *went in*(to) the war zone.
- (4) The students didn't *go in* for the long homework assignment.

Go off (inseparable): 1. Used to express a sudden loud reaction as in, for example: *The bomb went off early in the morning.* 2. When a plan or an event occurs as planned as in, for example:

*The school dance was fun, it **went off** well.* 3. To stop operating as in this example: *The light **went off** after the big storm hit.*

More examples:
- (1) My alarm ***went off*** at 3:30am by accident.
- (2) The fund raising event ***went off*** well. We collected over $2,000!
- (3) The refrigerator ***went off*** and all of the food spoiled.

Go on (inseparable): 1. Continue, as in the example: *I can't **go on** working at this job.* 2. To initiate operation of something, as in this example: *After the storm, the lights **went on** again.* 3 Used to inquire about what happened, as in this example: *What **went on** in class yesterday, I couldn't be there.* 4. To initiate some action, like, for example: *Silvia went on a diet yesterday.* 5. Can be used as encouragement, as in this example: ***Go on**, give it a try, I think you'll like this kind of food.*

More examples:
- (1) We couldn't ***go on*** paying the employee because he wasn't doing his job.
- (2) The refrigerator ***went on*** when we turned on the main electrical breaker.
- (3) What ***went on*** at the business meeting this morning?
- (4) We ***went on*** a two-day hike in the mountains.
- (5) ***Go on**,* you can win that game.

Go out (inseparable): 1. To leave or exit someplace, as in this example: *During the exam, no one was allowed to **go out** of the* *room.* 2. To stop burning or illuminating, as in this example: *all of the lights **went out** when the storm hit.* 3. Used to express what people do for leisure or romantic situations, as in this example: *My boyfriend and I **went out** last night and saw a movie.*

More examples:
- (1) I ***went out*** and smoked a cigarette during the movie.
- (2) The fire ***went out*** when it started raining.
- (3) My wife and I ***went out*** and had dinner.

Go over *(inseparable):* 1. Moving from one place to another place, as in this example: *My sister wants to go to Mary's house. Do you mind if I **go over** there with her?* 2. Used when expressing movement from one place to another place which usually is a home or familiar-feeling location, as in this example: *Last night we **went over** to the Yamaguchi's house for dinner;* 3. To review, as in this example: *Let's **go over** the exam and see where you made your mistakes.* 4. Used to express approval, as in this example: *Our financial report **went over** very well and the boss took us all out to dinner.*

More examples:
- (1) I ***went over*** to the other side of the room so I could hear the teacher better.
- (2) My wife and I ***went over*** to our daughter's house last night.
- (3) The colleagues ***went over*** the report before having the meeting.
- (4) His resume (CV) ***went over*** very well with the company.

Page 82

Go through (inseparable): 1. To commit to an action, usually in a difficult situation, as in this example: *We **went through** with the adoption of the child even though we knew the child was sick.*
- **More examples:**
  - (1) I just ***went through*** a divorce that was very difficult.
  - (1) We just ***went through*** two weeks of rainy weather and now we are ready for sunshine!

Go up (inseparable): 1. Moving to a higher place or to a place that is located north of your location, as in this example: *We **went up** to New York for our vacation (from Virginia). I **went up** the stairs to the second floor.* 2. Used to express increase in value or quality, as in this example: *Wow, the gas prices really **went up**!* 3. To approach something or someone, as in this example: *She **went up** to her teacher and asked when the exam was going to be given.*
- **More examples:**
  - (1) Claudia ***went up*** to Canada for a vacation (from New York).
  - (2) The price of food ***went up*** because the price of fuel went up.
  - (3) I ***went up*** to the tour guide and asked a question about the old building.

Go with (inseparable): 1. To compliment, one thing with another, as in this example: *Kaori bought a blouse to **go with** her skirt.* 2. To accompany, as in this example: *The chaperones **went** *with* the students to the dance. 3. To accept something or someone, or support someone or someone's idea or action, as in this example: *We had a choice between the red car and the green one, and we **went with** the red one. I'll go with Jane for class president.*

> **More examples:**
> - (1) Denise was shopping for a purse that would ***go with*** her black shoes.
> - (2) In an American breakfast, eggs usually ***go with*** bacon.
> - (3) We ended up ***going with*** the blue car because the red car was too big for us.

Goof around *(inseparable):* 1. To not take something seriously, or, having aimless fun; can also mean wasting time doing foolish things, as in this example: *He hasn't finished his work yet because he has been **goofing around** all day.*

> **More examples:**
> - (1) The students who ***goof around*** usually don't learn English very quickly.
> - (1) ***Goofing around*** is the fastest way to get fired from a job.

Gross out *(separable):* 1. Used to express causing to be disgusted or sickened by something or someone, as in this example: *He **grossed out** everyone at the table when he spit his food back onto his plate.*

> **More examples:**

- (1) We saw a dead cat in the road and it really *grossed* us *out*.
- (1) The toilet facilities were very dirty; they really *grossed* me *out*.

Grow out (separable): 1. To become too mature or old for a certain thing, behavior, or way of acting, as in this example: *Kazu couldn't fit into his high school clothes any more; he's **grown out** of them.* 2. When a person becomes too physically big to wear certain clothing, as in this example: *Our children are growing quickly, they have already **grown out** of all of their clothing and now we have to buy all new clothing.*

More examples:
- (1) My children are *growing out* of playing with dolls. Now they want more expensive toys.
- (2) This dress is too tight for me; it looks like I *have grown out* of this dress and I will have to buy a new one.

Grow up (inseparable): 1. A request by someone that someone acts more mature, as in this example: *Please **grow up** and act your age!* 2. To become older in age, as in this example: *Silvia **grew up** in California and now lives in Hawaii.*

More examples:
- (1) I wish you would *grow up* and accept the responsibilities that you have.
- (2) I *grew up* in New York and now live in Philadelphia.

Chapter 4 review

*Phrasal verbs beginning with the letter **G***

*Instructions: read and /or listen carefully to the sentences below. Fill in the blank spaces with the correct **preposition, particle,** or **adverb**. The answers can be found in this chapter (above).*

1. The couple living in the old house is able to get _____ on their pension checks.

2. It is difficult to get _____ if you don't work hard.

3. I'll do my homework when I get _____ to it.

4. To get _____ to our hotel we had to take a taxi.

5. Cancer research is important so my family got _____ the Cancer Society when they asked for volunteers.

6. Driver, I would like to get _____ at 23rd Street.

7. We told the Taxi drive to stop on Broadway. Then we got ____ of the taxi and went to a theater.

8. She got ____ the table and started dancing.

9. I really get ____ on doing math.

10. I borrowed a bicycle from my friend and, two days later, I gave it _____.

11. Everyone had to give ___ his or her exam after one hour.

12. We gave ___ the idea of going to Asia.

13. We went _____ with the competition even though it was raining.

14. Marco went _____ all day with two different colored socks on.

15. Go three stores _____ the restaurant and you will find the bookstore.

16. The electrical generator went _____ and the town didn't have electricity.

17. When you are taking an exam, time seems to go ___ too quickly.

18. The fire went _____ when it started raining.

19. When I asked where Kazu was, his colleagues told me that he went _____ to New York.

20. I grew ___ in New York and now live in Philadelphia.

Chapter 5
Phrasal verbs beginning with the letter H

In this section you will learn how to use many different phrasal verbs that begin with the letter H correctly in a sentence.

There are two kinds of phrasal verbs, separable and inseparable. Separable phrasal verbs can take an object between the verb and the preposition. For example: *My father **picked** me **up** after school and drove me home.* Inseparable phrasal verbs cannot take an object between the verb and the preposition. For example: I asked my friends to **come along** with me to the Christmas party. **Come along** cannot be separated by an object.

The numbers in front of the examples that are in parenthesis (), correspond the to number of the explanation found directly above. So, for example: 1. *explanation* . . . refers to (1) *example* . . . . If there is only one explanation or meaning given for the phrasal verb, then there will be two examples given for the one explanation. Both examples will be marked with (1).

If you have the accompanying Focus on English mp3 audio book (available separately from the school store or from www.FOEBooks.com) listen to each of the phrasal verbs, followed by their meanings and then some examples of how they are used in real English sentences. Each example will be spoken twice. There will be a review at the end of this chapter.

There will be a review at the end of this chapter.

Phrasal verbs beginning with the letter H

Hand back (separable):   1.   To return something, as in this example: *The teacher **handed back** the exams.*
>   **More examples:**
>   - (1) The customs official ***handed back*** my passport.
>   - (1) The sales clerk ***handed*** me ***back*** my change.

Hand in (separable):   1.   To give something to someone or a group that was expected, as, for example, in this sentence: *The students **handed in** their homework assignments. The applicants **handed in** their forms when they completed them.* 2. When you are quitting a job, sometimes you say you are ***handing in*** your resignation or your letter of resignation, as in this example: *I didn't like my job, so I **handed in** my resignation to my boss.*
>   **More examples:**
>   - (1) When we finished the exam, we ***handed*** it ***in*** to the teacher.
>   - (2) The manager ***handed in*** his letter of resignation on Friday.

Hand out (separable):   1.   To distribute, as in this example: *The student **handed out** the forms for the other students to complete.*
>   **More examples:**
>   - (1) The teacher ***handed out*** the corrected exams.
>   - (1) The man on the sidewalk ***handed out*** advertising to people who walked by.

Hand over (separable): 1. To release, give or relinquish to another, as in this example: *The police told the criminal that he had to **hand over** his gun.*
> **More examples:**
> - (1) The customs official asked the tourist to **hand over** her passport.
> - (1) The principal of the school told the student to **hand over** her cigarettes.

Hang around (inseparable): 1. To spend time idly or to loiter, as in this example: *We **hung around** the coffee shop talking about school.* 2. To keep company (with), to consort, as in this example: *The four friends have **hung around** together for ten years.*
> **More examples:**
> - (1) The students **hung around** the pizza parlor after school.
> - (2) The two sisters **hang around** together like best friends.

Hang on (inseparable): 1. To wait, as in this example: *I asked the customer to **hang on** while I looked for her size*; often used in telephone conversations, as in this example: *Hello. Mr. Liu? Yes, he is here, please **hang on** while I connect you.* 2. To grab onto or cling tightly to something or someone, as in this example: *The wind was very strong, I had to **hang onto** my umbrella.*
> **More examples:**
> - (1) **Hang on**; you've taken the wrong luggage out of the baggage claim area!

- (2) The amusement park ride was fun. We had to *hang on* really tightly!

Hang out *(separable):* 1. Similar meaning to *hang around* (above): to spend time idly or to loiter, as in this example: *We **hung out** at the coffee shop talking about school.* 2. Can also mean to keep company (with) or to consort (with), as in this example: *The four friends have **hung out** with each other for years.* 3. To suspend something or someone from something usually for the purpose of drying, as in this example: *The housewife **hung** the clothes **out** to dry.*

More examples:
- (1) Students often ***hang out*** at the local Internet cafe.
- (2) The friends ***hung out*** with each other after school.
- (3) We ***hung*** the wet towel ***out*** to dry on the clothesline.

Hang up *(separable):* 1. To finish a phone conversation, as in this example: *She **hung up** the phone after talking to her friend for an hour.* 2. To cause to delay, as in this example: *The bad traffic in the city **hung** us **up** for at least two hours.*

More examples:
- (1) The secretary ***hung up*** the phone after giving the customer travel directions to the office.
- (2) On Friday we were ***hung up*** in Houston because of a flight delay.

Have on *(separable):* 1. To wear something, as in this example: *The woman **had on** a beautiful black dress.*

More examples:
- (1) The secretary *had* a blue dress *on*.
- (1) The cat *had* a little cat sweater *on*.

Head back (inseparable): 1. To return, as in this example: *We headed back to the city after spending 5 hours in the country.*
More examples:
- (1) After spending a day at the beach, we *headed back* home.
- (1) We *headed back* to our home country after studying English in America.

Head for (inseparable): 1. To go towards, as in this example: *We got in our car and headed for the night club.* 2. You can also use this phrase to mean going towards a situation or consequence, as in this example: *Playing with that poisonous snake is a bad idea; he is headed for trouble.*
More examples:
- (1) On our vacations we usually like to *head for* the mountains.
- (2) If he keeps doing well on his exams, he is *headed for* top honors at his school.

Head off (separable): 1. To block the progress of something or someone, intercept or to block the completion of, as in this example: *When the water pipe broke we turned off the main water valve to head off more damage to the house.*
More examples:

- (1) The soldiers *__headed off__* the enemy before they got to the city.
- (1) The police *__headed off__* the thief before he could jump over the fence.

__Head towards__ *(inseparable):* 1. Similar to *head for* with the meaning going in the direction of, as in this example: *I asked the taxi driver to __head towards__ the center of town.*
More examples:
- (1) After work, we *__headed towards__* our favorite pub for some beer and conversation.
- (1) This country is *__headed towards__* disaster if that politician wins the election.

__Hear about__ *(inseparable):* 1. To learn of, or to get information concerning something or someone, usually verbally transmitted, as in this example: *Did you __hear about__ the big sale down at the mall? Yes, I __heard about__ it on the news.*
More examples:
- (1) Everyone *__heard about__* the big traffic accident.
- (1) I *__heard about__* the new tax that we will have to pay next year.

__Hear of__ *(inseparable):* 1. Similar in meaning to *hear about* but is commonly used between speakers attempting to identify something specifically, as in this example: *Did you ever __hear of__ a pillow tax? No, what __kind of__ tax is this?*
More examples:
- (1) Did you ever *__hear of__* the number 56 train?

- (1) Have you ever *heard of* Sally Little? No, I have never *heard of* her. Where is she from?

Heat up (separable): 1. To make hotter or warmer, as in this example: *The car was really cold, so we turned on the heater to heat the car up.* 2. Also used to mean make more intense, agitated, or more competitive, as in this example: *The contest has begun to heat up with the three top competitors all in the same round.*

> **More examples:**
> - (1) If you put some wood on the fire it will *heat up* the room.
> - (2) The conversation between the two men *heated up* and then someone called the police when the men started fighting.

Help out (separable): 1. To provide assistance to, as in this example: *We offered to help the old woman out with her shopping.*

> **More examples:**
> - (1) The daughter *helped* her mom *out* in the kitchen.
> - (2) Many people from the community came to *help out* the poor family.

Hit on (inseparable): 1. To arrive at an idea, conclusion, or solution, as in this example: *After days of thinking about the problem we finally hit on a solution.*

> **More examples:**
> - (1) The problem was complicated but we *hit on* a solution after talking about it for two days.

- (1) The chef *hit on* just the right combination of ingredients to make a delicious pasta dinner.

Hold against (inseparable): 1. To restrain or contain something or someone by forcing or pressing them against an object, as in this example: *The police held the robber against the wall while they searched his pockets for a gun.* 2. To blame, to be upset with someone or something for some wrongdoing, as in this example: *My business partner ruined our business, something I've always held against him.*
  More examples:
  - (1) The woman *held* her purse tightly *against* her side as she walked through the bad area of town.
  - (2) I was absent from the important meeting and my boss *held* that *against* me for a long time.

Hold off (separable): 1. To prevent or delay something from happening, as in this example: *We decided to hold off making our travel plans until after the summer.* 2. To keep at a distance, to resist, as in this example: *We held the reporters off by telling them that we had no comment.*
  More examples:
  - (1) The teacher *held off* giving the exam because some students needed more time to prepare.
  - (2) The actress's bodyguard *held off* the paparazzi while the actress got into the car.

Hold on (inseparable): 1. To cling or maintain one's grip, as in this example: *The amusement park ride was scary; we had to hold on* with both hands! 2. To persist or continue, as in this example: *The plane ride was long, but we **held on** and tried to relax until the plane finally landed.*

More examples:
- (1) The passenger **held on** to the handrail as the train came to a stop.
- (2) Our soccer team **held on** until the final minute but lost by one point.

Hold out (inseparable): 1. To continue to resist, as in this example: *The Indians attacked the fort but the soldiers in the fort were able to **hold out** for four more days.* 2. To refuse to reach an agreement, as in this example: *The employees wanted more money, but the management **held out** against their demand.* 3. To present or show, usually as proof of something, as in this example: *The politician said that health care was improving and to prove this he **held out** the new hospital as an example.*

More examples:
- (1) The soldiers were outnumbered by the enemy, but they **held out** until help arrived.
- (2) The workers would not go back to work. They were **holding out** for more benefits.
- (3) The company **held out** the possibility that workers would get an extra holiday with pay if they went back to work.

Hold over (inseparable): 1. To remain the same from an earlier time, as in this example: *The music was a **hold over** from the baroque period.* 2. To suspend, as in this example: *They **held*** the marshmallows *over* the fire to warm them up. 3. To continue or prolong, as in this example: *The movie was held over for an additional two weeks.*

More examples:
- (1) This custom is a ***hold over*** from ancient times.
- (2) She ***held*** the pot ***over*** the fire to heat up the potatoes.
- (3) The sale was ***held over*** for another week.

Hold up *(separable):* 1. To obstruct or delay, as in this example: *The work was **held up** because we did not have the correct materials.* 2. To rob someone, usually with a weapon, as in this example: *The thief **held up** the tourists and took all of their money.* 3. To continue to function under duress or pressure, as in this example: *The survivors **held up** well during their week without food.*

More examples:
- (1) The exam was ***held up*** because one of the exam sheets was missing.
- (2) The bank was ***held up*** yesterday. The thieves got more than $10,000.
- (3) The woman did not ***hold up*** well after surviving the storm with no food or water, and had to be hospitalized.

Hook up *(separable):* 1. To connect to, as in this example: *The fireman **hooked up** the water hose to the fire hydrant.* 2. (informal) To meet, make a new contact, or join, as in this example: *I needed to learn English faster, so I **hooked up** with a good English* *tutor*. 3. To assemble a mechanism with wiring, as in this example: *The electrician **hooked up** our wall socket in the kitchen.*

> **More examples:**
> - (1) The worker ***hooked up*** the new washing machine to the water system.
> - (2) We ***hooked up*** with some new friends when we studied English abroad.
> - (3) The electrician ***hooked up*** the dishwasher to the electrical mains.

Hurry up *(separable):* 1. Often used as a command to demand that someone go faster, as in this example: ***Hurry up****! The movie is going to start in three minutes!* 2. To hasten something, or make something or someone go faster, as in this example: *The teacher wanted the students to work faster on the practice exam, so he **hurried** them **up** by telling them they only had two minutes left to finish.*

> **More examples:**
> - (1) ***Hurry up****!* Class starts in five minutes.
> - (2) We ***hurried*** our project ***up*** by eliminating some of the less important items.

Chapter 5 review

*Phrasal verbs beginning with the letter **H***

*Instructions: read and /or listen carefully to the sentences below. Fill in the blank spaces with the correct **preposition, particle,** or **adverb**. The answers can be found in this chapter (above).*

1. The customs official handed _____ my passport.

2. The manager handed ___ his letter of resignation on Friday.

3. The customs official asked the tourist to hand _____ her passport.

4. The two sisters hang _____ together like best friends.

5. We hurried ___ our project by eliminating some of the less important items.

6. The electrician hooked ___ the dishwasher to the electrical mains.

7. The bank was held ___ yesterday. The thieves got more than $10,000.

8. The sale was held _____ for another week.

9. The actress's bodyguard held ____ the paparazzi while the actress got into the car.

10. Our soccer team held ___ until the final minute but lost by one point.

11. The workers would not go back to work. They were holding ___ for more benefits.

12. Many people from the community came to help ____ the poor family.

13. Did you ever hear ___ the number 56 train?

14. The soldiers headed ___ the enemy before they got to the city.

15. After spending a day at the beach, we headed _____ home.

16. The secretary had a blue dress _____.

17. On Friday we were hung ___ in Houston because of a flight delay.

18. If he keeps doing well on his exams, he is headed _____ top honors at his school.

19. This country is headed _____ disaster if that politician wins the election.

20. The woman held her purse tightly _____ her side as she walked through the bad area of town.

Chapter 6

*Phrasal verbs beginning with the letter **K***

In this section you will learn how to use many different phrasal verbs beginning with the letter K correctly in a sentence.

There are two kinds of phrasal verbs, separable and inseparable. Separable phrasal verbs can take an object between the verb and the preposition. For example: *My father **picked** me **up** after school and drove me home.* Inseparable phrasal verbs cannot take an object between the verb and the preposition. For example: I asked my friends to ***come along*** with me to the Christmas party. ***Come along*** cannot be separated by an object.

The numbers in front of the examples that are in parenthesis (), correspond the to number of the explanation found directly above. So, for example: 1. *explanation* . . . refers to (1) *example* . . . . If there is only one explanation or meaning given for the phrasal verb, then there will be two examples given for the one explanation. Both examples will be marked with (1).

If you have the accompanying Focus on English mp3 audio book (available separately from the school store or from www.FOEBooks.com) listen to each of the phrasal verbs, followed by their meanings and then some examples of how they are used in real English sentences. Each example will be spoken twice. There will be a review at the end of this chapter.

There will be a review at the end of this chapter.

Phrasal verbs beginning with the letter K

Read and /or listen carefully to the examples, as they will give you a good idea as to how to use the phrasal verb in real English sentences.

Keep at (*inseparable*): 1. To continue or persist at something, as in this example: *Building the home was difficult, but we **kept at** it until we were done.*
- **More examples:**
  - ❑ (1) Just ***keep at*** it! You'll get it done soon.
  - ❑ (1) The children made a castle in the sand; they ***kept at*** it all day.

Keep away (*separable*): 1. To deliberately maintain a distance from someone or something, as in this example: *The tour group was told to **keep away** from the edge of the cliff.*
- **More examples:**
  - ❑ (1) ***Keep away*** from that man because he is very dangerous.
  - ❑ (1) Children are told to ***keep away*** from alcohol.

Keep down (*separable*): 1. To diminish, suppress, or restrict from rising, as in these examples: *I can't eat chocolate any more because I am trying to **keep** my weight **down**. They are trying to **keep** the price of rice **down** but it has been difficult.*
- **More examples:**

❏ (1) Please *keep down* the noise; we are trying to study!

❏ (1) The child was sick and couldn't *keep* his food *down*. (Meaning that the child had to throw up a lot.)

Keep from (*separable*): 1. To prevent, sometimes under pressure, as in this example: *My love of chocolate keeps me from losing weight.*

More examples:
❏ (1) The heat in this room *keeps* me *from* thinking clearly.
❏ (1) That team's poor attitude *keeps* them *from* being number one.

Keep off (*separable*): 1. To stay clear of, to not stand, sit or lay on something, as in this example: *The sign said to keep off the grass because the ground was wet.*

More examples:
❏ (1) The mother told her child to *keep* her elbows *off* of the table.
❏ (1) We had to *keep off* the playing field because it was wet.

Keep on (*inseparable*): 1. To continue an action, as in this example: *We wanted to stop our car and look at the sunset but we had to keep on going because of the traffic.*

More examples:

- (1) Son, if you **_keep on_** tapping the table with your finger I'm going to get upset.
- (1) I was so tired, but I had to **_keep on_** running because the race was not over.

Keep to *(separable): 1.* To restrict to certain guidelines, as in this example: *During our vacation, we **kept** our spending **to** a minimum because we didn't have a lot of money.* 2. To guard as a secret, to restrict knowledge of something, as in this example: *I saw a strange object in the sky but I **kept** it **to** myself because I didn't want people to think I was crazy.*

More examples:
- (1) We played the radio but **_kept_** the noise **_to_** a minimum because students were studying in the next room.
- (2) I saw my friend's girlfriend with another boy but I **_kept_** it **_to_** myself because I didn't want my friend to be hurt.

Keep up *(separable):* 1. To maintain the condition of something, as in this example: *He **kept** his car **up** by washing and waxing it regularly.* 2. To carry on or persevere in something, as in this example: *Her foot was hurting her but she **kept up** with the other runners.* 3. To match the success of someone or something, as in this example: *Jennifer spent a lot of money to **keep up** with her friends. She has a nice car, nice clothes and a nice apartment.*

More examples:
- (1) He **_kept up_** the house by painting it.

- (2) The runner *kept up* his strong performance during the race.
- (3) We have a saying in English: Everyone is trying to *keep up* with the Jones.

The meaning of this saying is that everyone is trying to have all of the possessions and nice things that more successful families have.

Kick back (separable and inseparable depending on usage): 1. (separable) (slang) To give something, usually not ethical or legal, to someone for a favor, as in this example: *If you can get me a job with that company, I'll kick you back some cash.* 2. (inseparable) To recoil violently and usually unexpectedly, as in this example: *I fired the big rifle at the target, and it kicked back and hurt my shoulder.*

More examples:
- (1) The criminal *kicked back* some money to the police for not arresting him.
- (2) The soldiers fired the big cannon, which *kicked back* immediately.

Kick out (separable): 1. To reject, fire, get rid of, or remove someone or something from an organization or operation, as in this example: *We voted to kick that member out of the club because he was using drugs.* 2. (slang in the sport of surfing) Deliberately removing oneself from a wave, as in this example: *When she was done surfing on the wave so she kicked out.*

More examples:

- (1) They *kicked* him *out* of the bar because he was drunk.
- (2) The surfer *kicked out* of the wave just before it came crashing down.

Knock off (separable or inseparable depending on usage): 1. (separable) To forcibly remove someone or something from a position of being on top of something, as in this example: *The boy kicked the ball in the house and accidentally **knocked** the cook pot **off** of the stove.* 2. (informal) (inseparable) To take a break or rest, as in this example: *It's lunch time, lets **knock off**;* 3. (informal) (inseparable) To finish working, as in this example: *What time do you **knock off** work?* 4. (Informal) (separable) To rob or steal from, as in this example: *The bank robbers **knocked off** the local bank and got away with $10,000 cash.*

More examples:
- (1) The student accidentally *knocked* the book *off* of the desk.
- (2) The workers decided to *knock off* at ten for a cup of coffee.
- (3) I usually *knock off* work around 4:30pm.
- (4) The young thief *knocked off* the convenience store.

Knock out (separable): 1. To remove material from within material or an object, as in this example: *The construction workers **knocked out** a section of the wall to make room for a new window.* 2. To cause someone to lose consciousness, as in this example: *The boxer **knocked out** his opponent.* 3. (Informal) To finish a job quickly, as in this example: *It was an easy job; we **knocked** it **out** in an hour.* 4. To render useless, as in this example: *The lightening strike **knocked out** our electrical power.* 5. To exhaust oneself doing something, as in this example: *Stefan **knocked** himself **out** trying to finish the project before 10am.*

More examples:
- (1) The electrician **knocked out** a small hole in the wall to install a receptacle.
- (2) One fighter **knocked out** the other fighter in the championship match.
- (3) The homework wasn't difficult and I was able to **knock** it **out** in about 20 minutes.
- (4) The storm **knocked out** the power in the community.
- (5) Mei Ling really **knocked** herself **out** working on that project because she wanted to finish it before her vacation.

Knock over *(separable):* 1. To cause to tumble over or fall to the ground, as in this example: *The young boy **knocked over** the lamp while playing with his sister.*

More examples:
- (1) Keiko accidentally **knocked over** the orchid at the flower show.
- (1) The big football player easily **knocked over** his opponent.

Know about *(inseparable):* 1. To be familiar with, to have knowledge of, as in this example: *The students **knew about** the final exam date next week.*

    More examples:
- (1) The students ***knew about*** the problem the school was having with the bathrooms.
- (1) The visitor ***knew about*** the visa restrictions and had made plans to visit the country according to these restrictions.

Chapter 6 review

Phrasal verbs beginning with the letter **K**

Instructions: read and /or listen carefully to the sentences below. Fill in the blank spaces with the correct **preposition, particle,** *or* **adverb***. The answers can be found in this chapter (above).*

1. I was so tired, but I had to keep ___ running because the race was not over.

2. I saw my friend's girlfriend with another boy but I kept it ___ myself because I didn't want my friend to be hurt.

3. We had to keep ___ the playing field because it was wet.

4. That team's poor attitude keeps them _____ being number one.

5. The runner kept ___ his strong performance during the race.

6. I usually knock ___ work around 4:30pm.

7. They kicked him ___ of the bar because he was drunk.

8. The criminal kicked ___ some money to the police for not arresting him.

9. One fighter knocked ___ the other fighter in the championship match.

10. Please keep the noise ___; we are trying to study!

11. Children are told to keep ___ from alcohol.

12. Just keep ___ it! You'll get it done soon.

13. The big football player easily knocked ___ his opponent.

14. The students knew ___ the problem the school was having with the bathrooms.

15. The children made a castle in the sand; they kept ___ it all day.

Page 109

Chapter 7

*Phrasal verbs beginning with the letter **L***

In this section you will learn how to use many different phrasal verbs beginning with the letter L correctly in a sentence.

There are two kinds of phrasal verbs, separable and inseparable. Separable phrasal verbs can take an object between the verb and the preposition. For example: *My father **picked** me **up** after school and drove me home.* Inseparable phrasal verbs cannot take an object between the verb and the preposition. For example: I asked my friends to **come along** with me to the Christmas party. **Come along** cannot be separated by an object.

The numbers in front of the examples that are in parenthesis (), correspond the to number of the explanation found directly above. So, for example: 1. *explanation* . . . refers to (1) *example* . . . . If there is only one explanation or meaning given for the phrasal verb, then there will be two examples given for the one explanation. Both examples will be marked with (1).

If you have the accompanying Focus on English mp3 audio book (available separately from the school store or from www.FOEBooks.com) listen to each of the phrasal verbs, followed by their meanings and then some examples of how they are used in real English sentences. Each example will be spoken twice. There will be a review at the end of this chapter.

Page 110

There will be a review at the end of this chapter.

Phrasal verbs beginning with the letter L

Read and / or listen carefully to the examples, as they will give you a good idea as to how to use the phrasal verb in real English sentences.

Lay down (*separable*): 1. To put or place in a horizontal position, or in a position lower than the current position, as in this example: *The workers **laid** the window frame **down** so they could make some adjustments to the size.* 2. To specify rules, guidelines or parameters, as in this example: *The camp counselor **laid down** the rules to the young campers (meaning: the camp counselor explained the rules of the camp to the young campers).* 3. Used in expressing surrender of an opposition force, as in this example: *The enemy was told to **lay down** their arms and surrender.*

    More examples:
- (1) The student ***laid*** the papers ***down*** on the desk.
- (2) The immigration officer ***laid down*** the rules to the new visitors.
- (3) The crook was told to ***lay down*** his weapon and put his hands up.

Lay off (*separable or inseparable depending on usage*): 1. (*separable*) To terminate the employment of a worker, as in this example: *The company **laid** the workers **off** because of lack of work.*

2. *(inseparable) (slang)* Stop doing something, usually a forceful request to stop doing something, as in this example: ***Lay off**! Stop yelling at her. Can't you see that she is upset?*

More examples:
- (1) Five workers were ***laid off*** because the company was not making enough money.
- (2) ***Lay off*** alcohol because it makes you sick.

Lead up to *(inseparable):* 1. To proceed towards something, to lay the foundation for, as in this example: *The civil unrest and the burning of the flag all **led up to** the overthrow of the government.* 2. In books and movies, earlier parts of a story or article can lay a foundation for later parts, as in this example: *The first and second chapters of the book **led up to** the exciting events in the third chapter.*

More examples:
- (1) The health food store clerk told the girl that candy had a lot of sugar and bad chemicals in it. The clerk was ***leading up to*** the idea that candy is not good for you.
- (2) The first part of the movie ***led up to*** the climax in the middle of the movie.

Leave behind *(separable):* 1. To not take something or someone with you when moving to another location, as in this example: *When we moved to our new country, we had to **leave** all of our possessions **behind**.* 2. To advance ahead of others, as in this example: *One student in the class was so smart that he advanced quickly and he **left** the others **behind**.*

More examples:
- (1) When I left the theater, I *left* my purse *behind*.
- (2) I learned the material quickly, *left* the other students *behind*, and quickly rose to the top of my class.

Leave off (separable): 1. To stop temporarily, as in this example: *Okay class, we will **leave off** here in our reading and continue again tomorrow.*

More examples:
- (1) We stopped working on the project and went to lunch. When we get back, we'll pick up where we *left off* (meaning: we will continue working from the place where we *left off* when we went to lunch).
- (1) The teacher told the class that they would *leave off* at chapter ten and continue again tomorrow beginning with chapter 10.

Leave out (separable): 1. To omit, as in this example: *This chocolate cake doesn't taste right. I think we **left** out an ingredient.*

More examples:
- (1) We invited all of our friends to the party. We didn't *leave out* anyone.
- (1) Please study chapters three through seven but *leave out* chapter four.

Let down (separable): 1. To disappoint, as in this example: *Our soccer team really **let** us **down** by not winning that game!* 2. To lower something to a lower position gradually, as in this

Page 113

example: *The workers gently **let** the bundle of wood **down** until it reached the floor.*

> **More examples:**
> - (1) My daughter *let* me *down* when she got a bad grade on her exam.
> - (2) At the end of the day they *let down* the flag.

Let in *(separable):* 1. To admit, to allow something or someone enter, as in this example: *I hear someone knocking at the door; I'll let them in.*

> **More examples:**
> - (1) Please don't open the window because you'll *let* the mosquitoes *in*.
> - (1) It is never a good idea to *let* strangers *in*(to) your home.

Let in on *(inseparable):* 1. To include, usually other people, in sharing knowledge or ownership, as in this example: *Does Jim know the secret? No. Let's **let him in on** this.*

> **More examples:**
> - (1) I *let* my friend *in on* the secret about my new girlfriend.
> - (1) I think that it's a good time to *let* your colleagues *in on* this news.

Let off *(separable):* 1. To release from, as in this example: *The police officer stopped the man for speeding, but **let** him **off** (didn't give him a ticket) with a warning.* 2. Similar to *drop off*; to leave someone somewhere after riding on transportation, as in this example: *The taxi driver **let** me **off** at the library.* 3. To vent or release, as in this example: *The city **let off** fireworks for the Fourth of July celebrations.*

More examples:
- (1) The student didn't do his homework, but the teacher *let* him *off* because the student was sick.
- (2) The bus *let* him *off* in front of the bank.
- (3) The little boy *let off* his firecracker in the back yard.

Let out *(separable):* 1. To release, to release with permission, as in this example: *The principal **let** the students **out** of school during lunch break.* 2. To make bigger or larger as with clothing, as in this example: *As her children got a little older, their mother **let** the seams **out** of their clothing so that she would not have to buy new clothing so often.* 3. To release a noise, especially to express an emotion, as in this example: *When her boyfriend came up behind her and covered her eyes, she **let out** a scream.*

More examples:
- (1) The girl *let* her cat *out* of the house.
- (2) The seamstress *let out* the dress so it would fit the girl.
- (3) The cat *let out* a cry when I stepped on its tail.

Let up *(separable):* 1. To pause, as in this example: *The workers continued building the engine without **letting up**, because the deadline was very near.* 2. To release someone or something from a lower position, as in this example: *Okay, you win the wrestling match. Now **let** me **up**.*

More examples:
- (1) The rain didn't *let up* for even a minute.
- (2) The little girl in the swimming pool held her ball under water for a minute and then *let* it *up*.

Lie around (inseparable): 1. To lounge or rest without concern for anything in particular, as in this example: *What did you do last weekend? I just lay around and didn't do much of anything.* 2. A way to express disorganization especially when talking about possessions or items that usually belong in an area, as in this example: *He desk was a mess. There were folders and papers and office equipment lying around all over his desk.*

More examples:
- (1) During our vacation we just *lay around* and did nothing.
- (2) Papers were *lying around* everywhere and his room was really messy.

Lie down (inseparable): 1. To recline, as in this example: *The dog went over to his corner and lay down.*

More examples:
- (1) I went to my bedroom and *lay down* on the bed.
- (1) The dog was *lying down* next to the door.

Lift up (separable): 1. To raise something from a lower position to a higher position, as in this example: *We lifted up the hood of the car and looked at the motor.*

More examples:
- (1) The mother *lifted up* the little boy into her arms.

❑ (1) When I *lifted* the piece of wood *up*, there was a spider underneath.

Light up (separable): 1. To illuminate, as in this example: *We turned on the lights to **light up** the area.* 2. To become or cause to become cheerful or animated, as in this example: *She really **lit up** when her boyfriend asked her to marry him.* 3. To start smoking a cigarette or cigar, as in this example: *Let's go outside and **light up** (a cigarette).*

More examples:
❑ (1) The moon was so bright that it *lit up* the sky.
❑ (2) When I asked my friend to go to the concert with me, she really *lit up*.
❑ (3) Workers are not permitted to *light up* in the building.

Line up (separable): 1. To arrange things or people in a line, or to form a line, as in these examples: *I **lined up** the coins on the table and counted them. We **lined up** to buy tickets for the show.* 2. To arrange for or to arrange, as in this example: *We planned to have a festival in six months, so we **lined up** the location, food vendors, and equipment that we would need to have a successful festival.* 3. To align one thing with another thing, as in this example: *We have two boxes with a hole in each corner of each box. You have to place one box on top of the other box and **line up** the holes in the top box with the holes in the bottom box.*

More examples:
❑ (1) The people *lined up* to buy tickets..

Page 117

- (2) We have to *line up* our flight and accommodations for our vacation in six weeks.
- (3) The men building the new section of road *lined up* the new section with the old section.

Live with (inseparable): 1. To cohabitate, or to reside at the same location as someone or something, as in this example: *I live with my parents.* 2. To endure something that usually not pleasant or agreeable, as in this example: *My brother has been living with his disease for ten years.*

More examples:
- (1) My grandmother *lives with* my parents.
- (2) We have to *live with* the noise coming from that construction site every day.

Lock in (separable): 1. This term is often used in finances and investing and means to commit to an investment or financial transaction at a certain price, usually by giving money, as in this example: *I just bought stocks in a manufacturing company and I locked in at $56 per share.* 2. To close in and secure by lock, as in this example: *I was not allowed to bring my dog into the store, so I opened the car windows a little and locked my dog in the car.*

More examples:
- (1) When we bought our new house we *locked in* a mortgage at an interest rate of 2.5%.
- (2) My father *locked* his tools *in* the shed.

Lock out (separable): 1. To keep someone out of an area by means of securing by lock the entrance, as in this example: *I* *left the keys in my car and accidentally **locked** myself **out**.* 2. To withhold work from employees during a labor dispute, as in this example: *The company **locked out** its employees because of a disagreement about wage and benefits.*

> **More examples:**
> - (1) In my class, the teacher will **lock** you **out** of the classroom if you are late.
> - (2) The clothing company **locked out** its sewing machine operators because of a disagreement with their union about pay.

Lock up *(separable)*: 1. To secure by lock in a, for example, box, room, building, or institution, something or someone to prevent escape or to protect valuables, as in these examples: *We **locked up** the diamonds in the bank vault. The police locked the criminal up in jail.*

> **More examples:**
> - (1) The clerk **locked up** his store and went home at the end of the day.
> - (1) The woman **locked up** her car and went shopping in the mall.

Look around *(inseparable)*: 1. To use your vision and to turn your head in different directions to see things on different sides of you, as in this example: *I **looked around** to see where that loud noise came from.* 2. Often used when shopping for something or when searching for something. To first go here and then go there to try to find something or someone, as in this example: *I **looked around** for the best price for a new car.*

More examples:
- (1) When we arrived at the parking lot, we *looked around* for a parking spot.
- (2) Before purchasing a new house, we decided to *look around* and see what was available.

Look at (inseparable): 1. To focus with your eyesight on something or someone, as in this example: *We looked at the sunrise as we stood on the beach together.* 2. Used in expressing opinion or point of view, as in this example: *The way I look at it, we should not have spent all of our money on gambling.* 3. Sometimes used informally to talk about how much of something in an estimate, as in this example: *How much do you think the house will cost? I think you're looking at approximately $200,000.*

More examples:
- (1) When I asked the clerk for a discount, he *looked at* me as if I was crazy.
- (2) The two groups agreed on the idea; they both *looked at* it the same way.
- (3) The policeman told me that I was *looking at* a $500 fine for speeding.

Look down on (inseparable): 1. To regard with contempt or condescension, as in this example: *The rich people in the neighborhood looked down on their poorer neighbors.*

More examples:
- (1) The company manager *looked down on* the idea of giving someone a raise for no reason.

❏ (1) The two girls *looked down on* other girls who didn't wear current fashions.

Look for *(inseparable):* 1. To search for, to seek, as in this example: *I looked for my car keys, but I could not find them.*
   More examples:
   ❏ (1) The children *looked for* hidden gifts during the treasure hunt.
   ❏ (1) We drove along the coastline *looking for* a hotel.

Look forward to *(inseparable):* 1. To anticipate something in the future, usually in a positive way, as in this example: *I am looking forward to my vacation.*
   More examples:
   ❏ (1) The children *looked forward to* opening their presents.
   ❏ (1) We *looked forward to* resting after the long drive.

Look into *(inseparable):* 1. To research, to investigate, as in this example: *My wife and I were looking into buying a house in another country.*
   More examples:
   ❏ (1) The students are *looking into* attending school in Hawaii.
   ❏ (1) We *looked into* renting an apartment downtown, but it's too expensive.

Look out (inseparable): 1. To use caution, to be vigilant, as in this example: *This is a wonderful hike through the jungle, but you have to **look out** for snakes.*
> **More examples:**
> - (1) ***Look out**!* Stop the car! The road ends just ahead.
> - (1) Our bird watching group was ***looking out*** for brightly-colored birds.

Look over (separable): 1. To review something or someone carefully, as in this example: *The businessman **looked over** the contract before signing it.*
> **More examples:**
> - (1) We ***looked over*** the apartment before renting it.
> - (1) My girlfriend and I ***looked over*** the display of jewelry before making a selection.

Look up (separable): 1. To search for and find, as in a reference book, as in this example: *I took out my dictionary and **looked up** the meaning of the English word.*
> **More examples:**
> - (1) We ***looked up*** the telephone number in the directory.
> - (1) When I went to New York, I ***looked up*** an old friend.

Look up to (inseparable): 1. To admire, to respect, as in this example: *The people of the town **looked up to** Kimo because he was a successful, generous and kind man.*
> **More examples:**

- ❏ (1) The young worker *looked up to* his boss.
- ❏ (1) The violinist *looked up to* her teacher.

Luck out *(inseparable):* 1. To have good fortune, as in this example: *Boy, he really lucked out; he won the lottery!*
  More examples:
  - ❏ (1) He *lucked out* and got a good job.
  - ❏ (1) The thief *lucked out* and escaped the police.

Chapter 7 review

Phrasal verbs beginning with the letter L

Instructions: read and /or listen carefully to the sentences below. Fill in the blank spaces with the correct **preposition, particle,** *or* **adverb***. The answers can be found in this chapter (above).*

1. Please don't open the window because you'll let the mosquitoes ___.

2. The bus let him ___ in front of the bank.

3. I let my friend ___ on the secret about my new girlfriend.

4. My daughter let me ___ when she got a bad grade on her exam.

5. We invited all of our friends to the party. We didn't leave ___ anyone.

6. When I left the theater, I left my purse _____.

7. The first part of the movie led ___ to the climax in the middle of the movie.

8. In my class, the teacher will lock you ____ of the classroom if you are late.

9. My father locked his tools ___ the shed.

10. The woman locked ___ her car and went shopping in the mall.

11. When we arrived at the parking lot, we looked _____ for a parking spot.

12. We looked _____ renting an apartment downtown, but it's too expensive.

13. The policeman told me that I was looking ___ a $500 fine for speeding.

14. The two girls looked ____ on other girls who didn't wear current fashions.

15. The children looked ____ hidden gifts during the treasure hunt.

16. The children looked _____ ___ opening their presents.

17. We looked _____ the apartment before renting it.

18. The students are looking _____ attending school in Hawaii.

19. Look _____! Stop the car! The road ends just ahead.

20. We looked _____ the telephone number in the directory.

Chapter 8

*Phrasal verbs beginning with the letters **M, N, and O***

In this section you will learn how to use many different phrasal verbs beginning with the letter L correctly in a sentence.

There are two kinds of phrasal verbs, separable and inseparable. Separable phrasal verbs can take an object between the verb and the preposition. For example: *My father <u>picked</u> me <u>up</u> after school and drove me home.* Inseparable phrasal verbs cannot take an object between the verb and the preposition. For example: I asked my friends to <u>*come along*</u> with me to the Christmas party. <u>*Come along*</u> cannot be separated by an object.

The numbers in front of the examples that are in parenthesis (), correspond the to number of the explanation found directly above. So, for example: 1. *explanation* . . . refers to (1) *example* . . . . If there is only one explanation or meaning given for the phrasal verb, then there will be two examples given for the one explanation. Both examples will be marked with (1).

If you have the accompanying Focus on English mp3 audio book (available separately from the school store or from www.FOEBooks.com) listen to each of the phrasal verbs, followed by their meanings and then some examples of how they are used in real English sentences. Each example will be spoken twice. There will be a review at the end of this chapter.

There will be a review at the end of this chapter.

Phrasal verbs beginning with the letters M, N, and O

Read and / or listen carefully to the examples, as they will give you a good idea as to how to use the phrasal verb in real English sentences.

Make for (inseparable): 1. To create conditions or environment for a situation, action or event, as in this example: *This cool weather **makes for** very nice hiking.*
> **More examples:**
> - (1) The comfortable chair *made for* a nice place to sit and watch TV.
> - (1) The beautiful weather *made for* a nice day to go to the beach.

Make of (inseparable): 1. Interpret something, an event, action, or situation, as in this example: *Person A: What do you **make of** all of that smoke on the horizon? Person B: I think that there is a big fire in the bush.* 2. How something is built, or what something consists of, as in this example: *The house is **made of** wood.*
> **More examples:**
> - (1) When we first arrived in Rome we didn't know what to *make of* all the winding streets.
> - (1) The students didn't know what to *make of* the first part of the exam because it didn't have anything to do with the material they studied.
> - (2) The vase is *made of* glass.

Make out (inseparable or separable depending on usage): 1. (inseparable) To be successful at something, as in this example: _I made $20,000 on that investment; I really_ **made out** _well!_ 2. (separable) To be able to see and identify something, as in this example: _As we were approaching the city, I could just_ **make out** _the Empire State Building._ 3. (separable) To fill in, as with a form, application, check, etc., as in this example: _I paid my landlord for rent. I_ **made** _the check_ **out** _to his company._ (Meaning: _The name that I wrote on the check was the name of my landlord's company._) 4. (separable) To represent something or someone as being a certain way, as in this example: _The cake in that restaurant wasn't as bad as you_ **made** _it_ **out** _to be._

> **More examples:**
> - (1) We got the tickets at half price; we really **made out** well.
> - (2) Standing on the seashore, we could **make out** the outline of a ship far at sea.
> - (3) My wife **made** a check **out** for $1500 to pay the rent.
> - (4) The concert wasn't very good but my friend **made** it **out** to be fantastic.

Make up (inseparable or separable depending on usage): 1. To invent or create a story, explanation, or reason for something, sometimes used for deceitful purposes, as in this example: _My son_ **made up** _an excuse for why he didn't go to school today. Unfortunately, no one believed him._ 2. To do or complete something that should have been completed earlier, as in this example: _Sally didn't do her homework, so she had to_ **make** _it_ **up** *and give it to the teacher the next day.* 3. Comprised of or to be part of a larger something, group, or action, as in this example: *This drink is **made up** of soda and alcohol.* 4. To make a decision, as in this example: *I **made up** my mind to never go back to that restaurant.* 5. To put on cosmetics, as in this example: *The woman went into the rest room and **made** herself **up**.*

More examples:
- (1) I don't think that was the real reason why he quit the company. I think he *made* that *up*.
- (2) The teacher said that everyone who didn't take the exam yesterday has to *make* it *up* tomorrow.
- (3) The business group is *made up* of executives from different companies.
- (4) My boss *made up* her mind never to hire poorly qualified applicants.
- (5) The clown *made* himself *up* before the show.

Mess up (separable): 1. To make a mistake or error, as in this example: *I really **messed up** on my exam and my grade was low.* 2. To make dirty or disorganized, as in this example: *Stephan made a great meal but he really **messed up** the kitchen.*

More examples:
- (1) I really *messed up* the exam and ended up getting a low grade.
- (2) The child spent the day in his room and really *messed* it *up*.

Mix up (separable): 1. To confuse, as in this example: *I got really **mixed up** during the exam and got a poor grade.* 2. To blend two or more things together, as in this example: *We **mixed up** the ingredients for the cake, put them in a pan, and then baked them in an oven.*

> **More examples:**
> ❑ (1) I always ***mix up*** the names of the twin sisters.
> ❑ (2) ***Mix*** rice ***up*** with vegetables for a delicious meal.

Move in (inseparable or separable depending on usage): 1. (separable To begin to occupy a place of residence or business; usually you bring your furniture and personal belongings into the new location and then begin to occupy the new location, as in this example: *We **moved in**(to) our new home on the 4th of December.* 2. (inseparable To advance towards something, as in this example: *The enemy was **moving in** on the military camp.*

> **More examples:**
> ❑ (1) We are ***moving into*** our new business headquarters tomorrow.
> ❑ (2) The police ***moved in*** on the criminal hideout.

Move out (separable): 1. To leave a location, usually with belongings, equipment, or other things that may be important to you or a group, as in this example: *Our company **moved out** of the building and moved into a new, much larger building.*

> **More examples:**
> ❑ (1) We are ***moving out*** of our rental tomorrow.
> ❑ (1) The company is ***moving out*** of the city.

Narrow down (separable): 1. To reduce in size or in scope, as in this example: *We are going on vacation in two months but we* had to **_narrow down_** the list of things we wanted to do because we don't have enough time.

> **More examples:**
> - (1) The company **_narrowed down_** the list of applicants to just two.
> - (1) We **_narrowed down_** our choices to two: go to the beach or relax at home.

Open up *(separable):* 1. To remove a cover or top or to open a door to reveal something inside of an enclosed area, as in this example: *We **opened up** our gifts at the beginning of the holiday.* 2. To speak very honestly to someone because you trust them with certain information, as in this example: *I **opened up** to my teacher and told him why I am having trouble in class.* 3. To make available or accessible, as in this example: *The prime minister **opened up** his country for trade with the rest of the world.* 4. To spread out or unfold, as in this example: *The student **opened up** the book and read the paragraph.* 5. To begin operation, as in this example: *The store **opened up** last week and is having a big sale.*

> **More examples:**
> - (1) The young boy **_opened up_** the box and found a soccer ball inside.
> - (2) I **_opened up_** to my friend about my recent bad luck.
> - (3) The new corporation in our city **_opened up_** many opportunities for employment.
> - (4) We **_opened up_** the map and found our location.
> - (5) The school **_opened up_** two years ago and is already very popular with students.

Chapter 8 review

*Phrasal verbs beginning with the letters **M, N, and O***

*Instructions: read and /or listen carefully to the sentences below. Fill in the blank spaces with the correct **preposition, particle,** or **adverb**. The answers can be found in this chapter (above).*

1. The company is moving ____ of the city.

2. We are moving ____ our new business headquarters tomorrow.

3. Mix rice ____ vegetables for a delicious meal.

4. I really messed ____ the exam and ended up getting a low grade.

5. We opened ____ the map and found our location.

6. The company narrowed ____ the list of applicants to just two.

7. The clown made himself ____ before the show.

8. We got the tickets at half price; we really made ____ well.

9. When we first arrived in Rome we didn't know what to make ____ all the winding streets.

10. The beautiful weather made ____ a nice day to go to the beach.

Page 132

Chapter 9
*Phrasal verbs beginning with the letter **P***

Reminder: There are two kinds of phrasal verbs, separable and inseparable. Separable phrasal verbs can take an object between the verb and the preposition. For example: *My father **picked** me **up** after school and drove me home.* Inseparable phrasal verbs cannot take an object between the verb and the preposition. For example: I asked my friends to ***come along*** with me to the Christmas party. ***Come along*** cannot be separated by an object.

The numbers in front of the examples that are in parenthesis (), correspond the to number of the explanation found directly above. So, for example: 1. *explanation* . . . refers to (1) *example* . . . . If there is only one explanation or meaning given for the phrasal verb, then there will be two examples given for the one explanation. Both examples will be marked with (1).

If you have the accompanying Focus on English mp3 audio book (available separately from the school store or from www.FOEBooks.com) listen to each of the phrasal verbs, followed by their meanings and then some examples of how they are used in real English sentences. Each example will be spoken twice. There will be a review at the end of this chapter.

There will be a review at the end of this chapter.

Phrasal verbs beginning with the letter P

Pass on *(separable):* 1. To relay from one to another, as in this example: *When my mother died she **passed** her jewelry **on** to her daughters.* 2. To die; a polite way of saying that a person has died, as in this example: *Last night her grandfather **passed on**.*

More examples:
- (1) When my brother grew older, he ***passed*** his clothes ***on*** to his little brother.
- (2) My father ***passed on*** some years ago, but he left me with a wonderful education.

Pass out *(separable or inseparable depending on usage):* 1. *(separable)* To distribute something, as in this example: *The immigration officer **passed out** booklets explaining immigration law.* 2. *(inseparable)* To lose consciousness, as in this example: *It was so hot in the room that some people **passed out**.*

More examples:
- (1) The teacher ***passed out*** the exams.
- (2) The mountain climber ***passed out*** for lack of oxygen.

Pass over *(separable):* 1. To be left out, omitted, or disregarded as in this example: *Some of the employees at the company were **passed over** for a raise because they were too new.*

More examples:
- (1) During our vacation, we ***passed over*** going to Las Vegas because it was too expensive.

- (1) There was so much food at the buffet that we *passed over* on trying many things.

Pass up *(separable):* 1. To forego, to not accept, to let go, as in this example: *I **passed up** the chocolate cake for dessert because I was full.*
- **More examples:**
  - (1) I ***passed up*** an opportunity to go to France because I had to finish a project at work.
  - (1) I ***passed up*** the pudding at dinner last night; I heard it was good.

Pay back *(separable):* 1. To return something, usually a debt of some kind, as in this example: *Keone **paid** the bank **back** the money he borrowed from them.* 2. Retribution, sometimes used to express returning or giving something back for something negative received earlier, as in this example: *We **paid** the thief **back** by calling the police.*
- **More examples:**
  - (1) Christina ***paid back*** her credit card debt.
  - (2) I paid her ***back for*** starting that rumor.

Pay for *(inseparable):* 1. Remuneration, to exchange money or something of value for something else of value, as in this example: *Jeff **paid for** the groceries and left the store.* 2. Used to express retribution, to refer to the penalty you have to pay when you do something wrong, too much of something, too little of something etc., as in this example: *I ate way too much chocolate cake and now I am **paying for** it with a stomachache!*

More examples:
- (1) We traded the farmer some clothes to ***pay for*** the oranges he gave us.
- (2) People who break the law have to ***pay for*** it by going to jail.

Pay off *(separable):* 1. To finish paying for something, as in this example: *I finally **paid off** my car!* 2. Sometimes used to express bribery, or paying someone to do something that may not be legal or ethical, as in this example: *The music company **paid** the radio station **off** for playing their music on the radio.*

More examples:
- (1) We traded the farmer some clothes to ***pay for*** the oranges he gave us.
- (2) The lady driver tried to ***pay*** the police officer ***off*** for not giving her a ticket.

Pay up *(inseparable):* 1. To settle a debt or pay an amount of money that is demanded, as in this example: *Hey, you owe me $20; **pay up**!*

More examples:
- (1) My roommate told me that we needed to ***pay up*** our light bill or the electric company would turn off the electricity next week.
- (1) The bartender asked the group to pay for their tab: "***Pay up***, or I'll call the police."

Pick on *(inseparable):* 1. To tease or bully, as in this example: *My older brother always used to **pick on** me.*

More examples:
- (1) I don't know why the teacher always *picks on* me.
- (1) Mother: "Please don't *pick on* your little sister!"

Pick out (separable): 1. To choose or select, as in this example: *Mary went shopping and picked out a beautiful black dress.* 2. To discern or to distinguish from the surroundings, as in this example: *I picked the criminal out from a picture of twenty suspects.*

More examples:
- (1) I needed a new tie so I went to the clothing shop and *picked* one *out*.
- (2) While we watched the sun set over the ocean, I was able to *pick out* a sailboat far out at sea.

Pick up (separable): 1. To take something up by hand or by mechanical device as in this example: *The student picked up the book and put in on the desk.* 2. To clean up, as in this example: *Mom picked up the room after we left.* 3. To take on passengers or freight, as in this example: *The train picked up the passengers at 3pm.* 4. (informal) To acquire in a casual way, as in this example: *I picked up a CD at the record shop on my way home.* 5. To learn or to acquire knowledge (the feeling of this is meant to be casual and not formal), as in this example: *I pick up languages easily.* 6. Can be used to mean: claim something that you left behind, as in this example: *Kimo picked up his pants at the dry cleaners.* 7. To catch a disease or sickness, usually passed on from someone else, as in this example: *I picked up malaria while in the south of the country.* 8. To take

Page 137

into custody, or to capture (usually used with police or military), as in this example: *The police **picked up** the robber and took him to the police station.* 9. Casual relationship; used to express meeting someone in a casual environment like a bar, as in this example: *I **picked up** a girl at the pub last night.* 10. To encounter or come upon and observe, as in this example: *The ship **picked up** the enemy aircraft on their radar.* 11. To continue something after a break, as in this example: *Let's **pick** this discussion **up** after a lunch break.* 12. To improve a situation or condition, as in this example: *Her attitude really **picked up** after getting that good grade on the exam!* 13. (slang) To leave unexpectedly, as in this example: *He was so mad he just **picked up** and ran out of the room.*

More examples:
- (1) The crane *picked* up the old car and put it on a pile of old cars.
- (2) After the party we all helped to *pick up* the room.
- (3) The taxi *picked* us *up* at the train station.
- (4) I *picked up* some popcorn on the way to the party.
- (5) I'm good at math; I *pick* it *up* easily.
- (6) Kathryn gave the shoemaker her claim check so that she could *pick up* her shoes that were repaired.
- (7) My brother said that he *picked up* the flu on the flight from Houston to Cleveland.
- (8) The military police *picked up* the drunken sailors.
- (9) My friend told me he *picked up* two women last night.
- (10) The police *picked up* the speeder on their radar.

- (11) We *picked up* where we left off in our meeting after we had lunch.
- (12) Business really *picked up* after the holiday.
- (13) My girlfriend said that she *picked up* and left her boyfriend because of his abuses.

Pile up (separable): 1. To accumulate or amass things, as in this example: *My wife **piled up** all the books and took them back to the library.*

More examples:
- (1) Claudia *piled up* traffic tickets, mostly because she drove too fast.
- (1) Kelly loved ice cream. She *piled up* ice cream on her plate for dessert.

Piss off (separable) (slang): 1. To make angry, as in this example: *People who throw garbage out of their car window **piss** me **off**.*

More examples:
- (1) Kaori was *pissed off* that she got a poor grade on her exam.
- (1) The police officer was really *pissed off* and gave the guy a ticket for driving recklessly.

Plan ahead (inseparable): 1. To think about and organize for things that you would like to happen in the future, as in this example: *We would like to have a successful party next month so we are **planning ahead**.*

More examples:

- (1) The festival organizers *planned ahead* for the big celebration.
- (1) We wanted to avoid unpleasant surprises during our vacation so we *planned ahead* very carefully.

Plan for (inseparable): 1. To prepare for something, as in this example: *We planned for the long, cold winter season by cutting lots of wood for the fireplace.*
More examples:
- (1) We knew the company was going to lay us off; we *planned for* it.
- (2) We *planned for* the food shortage by storing lots of food on our shelves last year.

Plan on (inseparable): 1. To be prepared for or to anticipate something that will occur in the future, as in this example: *We planned on staying in school an extra hour.*
More examples:
- (1) When we went to the theater, we *planned on* waiting on a long line for tickets.
- (1) We *plan on* going to China next summer.

Play around (inseparable): 1. (informal) To be disloyal to a significant other, boyfriend, girlfriend, wife or husband in particular, as in this example: *My wife was playing around with another man; I'm going to ask for a divorce.* 2. (informal) To tinker with something without really understanding how it works, or what the nature of a problem is, as in this example: *The lawnmower stopped working so I played around with it for a while* to see if I could fix it. 3. (informal) To not be serious, joking, jesting, teasing, etc., as in this example: *I was only **playing around** with you when I said I didn't like your clothes.*

More examples:
- (1) I caught my boyfriend ***playing around*** with my best friend.
- (2) The car wouldn't start this morning so I ***played around*** with the battery until I got it started.
- (3) I hope my friend understands that I am only ***playing around*** when I brag about how good I am at that game.

Plug in (separable): 1. To connect an electrical to a wall receptacle, as in this example: *We **plugged in** the toaster so we could have breakfast.* 2. (slang) Used to talk about one's connection to, or one's awareness of information from a social or professional network, as in this example: *If you really want to be up to date in your field, you should be **plugged into** your professional association.*

More examples:
- (1) The workman ***plugged in*** the electric drill.
- (2) I'm ***plugged into*** the local gossip network so I know everything that's going on in this town.

Plug up (separable): 1. To stop and restrict the flow of something, as in this example: *The plumber temporarily **plugged up** the leak in the hose.*

More examples:

- (1) Hair and other things ***plugged up*** the shower drain.
- (2) The major roads into town were ***plugged up*** with traffic.

Point out *(separable)*: 1. To direct one's attention to something, as in this example: *The tour guide **pointed out** the 2000-year-old statue to the tourists.* 2. To stress or emphasize certain information to someone, as in this example: *The teacher **pointed out** to the students that the homework would be due next Tuesday.*

More examples:
- (1) The store clerk ***pointed out*** the casual blue dress to her customer.
- (2) I would like to ***point out*** to you that this is not the first time your son was caught cheating on an exam.

Point to *(inseparable)*: 1. To cause to focus one's attention on an area of concern, as in this example: *The unusual weather, the heavy rains, the melting ice all **point to** global warming as a possible cause.* 2. When you use your hand or finger to direct one's attention to something or someone, as in this example: *When the clerk in the candy store asked the boy what he wanted, the boy **pointed to** the red candy.*

More examples:
- (1) The student always looked out of the window and did not pay attention while in class, ***point to*** the fact that the student was not interested in the subject.
- (2) The boy's mother ***pointed to*** his bedroom and said, "Clean it up, now!"

Print out *(separable):* 1. To print by mechanical means something produced in a computer, as in this example: *The manager **printed out** his report after completing it on the computer.*
- ❏ (1) The student couldn't get his report to ***print out*** because there wasn't enough memory in the printer.
- ❏ (1) The office worker ***printed out*** the work schedule for the following month.

Pull off *(separable):* 1. *(informal)* To succeed at something despite difficult conditions, or low probability of success, as in this example: *I **pulled off** an A on the exam.*
More examples:
- ❏ (1) The workers moved a house from one state to another without damaging anything; everyone was surprised that they ***pulled*** it ***off***.
- ❏ (1) I can't believe that I ***pulled off*** that double back flip.

Pull out *(separable):* 1. To remove, sometimes with force, as in this example: I pulled the young boy out of the water. 2. To leave, or to vacate an area, as in this example: *The military **pulled out** of the area because it was finished with its operations.*
More examples:
- ❏ (1) The firemen ***pulled*** the woman ***out*** of the burning house.
- ❏ (2) The Navy ***pulled*** its ships ***out*** of the area because they were needed elsewhere.

Pull over (separable): 1. To drive a vehicle over to the side of the road, as in this example: *I **pulled** the car **over** to let the ambulance go by.*
> **More examples:**
> - (1) The policeman told me to **pull** my car **over** to the side of the road.
> - (1) The truck driver **pulled over** so he could check his tires.

Pull through (inseparable): 1. To recover from for survive something, as in this example: *My friend was sick for a month, but he finally **pulled through** and he's okay now.*
> **More examples:**
> - (1) The shipwrecked survivors **pulled through** the long ordeal, and they are recovering now in a hospital in New York.
> - (1) My sister **pulled through** a long bout with the flu.

Punch in (inseparable): 1. To register your time of entry to a job or other organization, usually with a time clock or other mechanical time-keeping device, as in this example: *We **punch in** at 8 o'clock every day at our company.*
> **More examples:**
> - (1) I **punched in** five minutes late yesterday; the boss wasn't happy about this.
> - (1) We usually **punch in** ten minutes early every day.

Punch out *(inseparable):* 1. To register your time of exit from a job or other organization, usually with a time clock or other mechanical time-keeping device, as in this example: *We **punched out** at 5 o'clock and then left the building.*

More examples:
- (1) We ***punched out*** early yesterday so we could go to the concert.
- (1) Jason ***punches out*** a 6pm every night; he's a hard worker.

Put away *(separable):* 1. To return something to a usual location, as in this example: *We **put** the books **away** back on the shelf.* (Note: when we use "back," in this context we mean "where something usually is located.") 2. (informal) Used to express eating large quantities of food or drink, as in this example: *Wow, you can really **put** it **away**! You've eaten two plates of food!* 3. To put someone in jail or to place someone in an mental institution, as in this example: *The murderer was **put away** for life.*

More examples:
- (1) After I looked at the new CD player the sales clerk ***put*** it ***away*** in the showcase.
- (2) Jack ***put*** two pizzas ***away***; now he's sick.
- (3) She was acting crazy so they ***put*** her ***away*** for a while. (Meaning: they put her in a mental institution.)

Put back *(separable):* 1. Similar to put away, to return something to a usual location, as in this example: *We **put** the* books *back* on the shelf. (Note: when we use "back," in this context we mean "where something usually is located.")

More examples:
- (1) After looking at the pictures in the book, I *put* it *back* on the shelf.
- (1) The mother said to the little boy: "Please *put* the cookie *back*; you're going to eat dinner in ten minutes!"

Put down (separable): 1. To take something you are holding and place it in a lower, sometimes horizontal, position, as in this example: *Katrina put the book down and walked to the white board.* 2. To criticize, as in this example: *I don't mean to put you down but your pants don't match your shirt.* 3. To make a partial payment on something, or a payment to hold something for future purchase, as in this example: *I bought the house. The bank asked me to put down $10,000 and they would lend me the rest of the money needed to purchase the house.* 4. To add something in writing to something else, like a list, as in this example: *I put down my name on the signup list.* 5. To attribute an action or occurrence to something else, as in this example: *The student failed the exam. He put it down to not studying enough.* 6. To land an aircraft, as in this example: *The passengers were surprised when the pilot announced he would put the plane down in a different city.*

More examples:
- (1) After playing with the baby, the father *put* it *down* in its bed.

- (2) All the children used to *put* her *down* for being so small.
- (3) I *put down* $50 so the store would hold the bicycle for me until I purchased it in June.
- (4) I *put* my full name *down* on the top of the exam.
- (5) I don't understand why people drink alcohol and then drive a car. I just *put* it *down* to stupidity.
- (6) The pilot *put* the plane *down* in New York.

Put in (separable): 1. To cause to make a formal offer, or to offer, as in this example: *Soo Woo put in an offer of $100,000 for the house.* 2. To contribute to, to add to, as in this example: *Each student put in $2 towards the purchase of the pizza.* 3. To arrive at a port, especially a commercial or military ship, as in this example: *The cruise ship put in at Pago Pago, American Samoa.* 4. To install something, as in this example: *The workers put in a new computer system for the company.* 5. To spend time, as in this example: *The employee put in thirty years at his company.*

More examples:
- (1) I *put in* a bid (offer) of $5000 for the blue car at the car auction.
- (2) We all *put in* $10 to help pay for the food at the party.
- (3) The military ship *put in* at Guam.
- (4) The government *put in* a new bridge over the river.
- (5) The criminal *put in* twenty years in jail for the robbery.

Put off (separable): 1. To delay or postpone something, as in this example: *Pablo **put off** going on vacation until all of his work was done.* 2. To repel or repulse, as in this example: *Joan's awkward behavior at the party **put** the other guests **off**.*

    More examples:
- (1) The teacher ***put off*** giving the exam today because there were too many students absent.
- (2) The dirty restaurant really ***put*** us ***off***.

Put on (separable): 1. To dress or put on clothes, or to apply something, as in this example: *Jeremy **put on** his jacket and left the house.* 2. (informal) To fool, tease or mislead in a playful way, as in this example: *My friends were **putting** me **on** when they told me they saw a ghost.* 3. To attach something to something, as in this example: *The Yorimoto family **put** a new addition **on**(to) their house.* 4. Can be used to talk about weight gain, as in this example: *I saw Sally the other day and it looked like she had **put on** some weight.*

    More examples:
- (1) Reiko ***put on*** her best perfume for the party.
- (2) My brother told me there were ten thousand people at the concert last night; he was ***putting*** me ***on***.
- (3) The librarian ***put*** the sticker ***on*** the book for identification.
- (4) My mother is a good cook and I think I ***put on*** some weight.

Put out *(separable)*: 1. To take something from inside of a close area and put it outside of the enclosed area, as in this example: *The garbage man is coming tomorrow morning, so we **put** the garbage **out** for him to pick up.* 2. To extinguish a fire or switch off a light, as in this example: *The firemen **put out** the house fire.* 3. To be inconvenienced or annoyed, as in this example: *I hope that we didn't put you out by our unexpected visit to your house.* 4. To distribute something like a magazine, newspaper, or printed advertising, as in this example: *The publishing company **put** the magazine **out** last May.*

More examples:
- (1) The bartender ***put*** the two boys ***out*** of the pub for being under age.
- (2) The mother asked her son to ***put out*** the lights in the living room before going to bed.
- (3) We were really ***put out*** by all of the road construction in front of our house.
- (4) We plan to ***put*** the advertising ***out*** in about a month.

Put past *(separable)*: 1. Used to express doubt and sometimes mistrust about the actions of someone, or to talk about someone's capacity to do something that is not quite right, as in this example: *I wouldn't **put** it **past** him to find a way to get his certificate without taking an exam, while the rest of us have to take the exam.*

More examples:
- (1) That guy has been in jail for theft before and I wouldn't ***put*** it ***past*** him to do steal again.

- (2) I wouldn't *put* it *past* mom to check on where we go at night.

Put to (*separable*): 1. Usually refers to placing some part of your body or something in your hand against something else in order to accomplish some action, as in this example: *I **put** my ear **to** the wall to listen to my neighbor's conversation.* 2. Used to express causing an inconvenience to someone else, as in this example: *Sorry to **put** you **to** the trouble, but may I use your phone?* 3. To confront with a question or information, as in this example: *We didn't know when we were going to get our grades, so I **put** that question **to** the teacher.*

More examples:
- (1) I *put* my pencil *to* paper and made a list of the things I needed for the trip.
- (2) They really *put* my brother *to* a lot of trouble when they asked him to help out with the fund raising.
- (3) When my friend *put* his idea *to* me that way, I could understand it better.

Put together (*separable*): 1. To assemble, or to build, as in this example: *My younger brother **put** the pieces **together** and completed the puzzle.* 2. To organize something, usually an event or activity, as in this example: *The students **put together** a nice party for all of the students in the school.* 3. To place in close proximity, or close together, as in this example: *The teacher **put** students from different countries **together** to practice their English.*

More examples:

- (1) We *put* the model airplane *together* in about four hours.
- (2) The town leaders *put together* a really nice Fourth of July celebration.
- (3) The teacher *put* the older students together and the younger students *together* to work on separate projects.

Put up (separable): 1. To provide accommodations or a place to stay, as in this example: *When my cousin arrived from Ohio, we put him up for a week.* 2. To build or construct something, as in this example: *The workers put up the house in a short time.* 3. To provide funds or funding in advance, as in this example: *The rich man put up the money to build the new art museum.* 4. To attach something to something else, like a notice on a bulletin board, as in this example: *The housewife put up the curtains on the window.* 5. To upload, especially website files, as in this example: *We put up our new website last Tuesday.* 6. To display, carry on, or engage in something, as in this example: *She really put up a good argument as to why she should be paid more money.*

More examples:
- (1) When my brother visited from Minnesota, I *put* him *up* for a week.
- (2) The construction company *put up* apartment buildings.
- (3) We had a good idea for a business, but we needed someone to *put up* the money to help us start it.
- (4) We *put up* signs all over town to advertise the loss of our dog.

- (5) We *put up* some files that added two more pages to our website.
- (6) The boxer *put up* a good fight, but lost the match in the third round.

Put up with (inseparable): 1. To tolerate something or someone, or be patient with an uncomfortable situation, as in this example: *The price for the hotel room was cheap so we **put up with** the bad service, noise, and uncomfortable bed.*

More examples:
- (1) We *put up with* the noise from the construction for a week.
- (1) The flight to Rome from Frankfurt was really cheap, so we *put up with* the uncomfortable seating on the aircraft.

Chapter 9 review

Phrasal verbs beginning with the letter **P**

Instructions: read and /or listen carefully to the sentences below. Fill in the blank spaces with the correct **preposition, particle,** *or* ***adverb***. *The answers can be found in this chapter (above).*

1. My roommate told me that we needed to pay ____ our light bill or the electric company would turn ____ the electricity next week.

2. We traded the farmer some clothes to pay ____ the oranges he gave us.

3. Christina paid _____ her credit card debt.

4. We traded the farmer some clothes to pay ____ the oranges he gave us.

5. Mother: "Please don't pick ___ your little sister!"

6. I needed a new tie so I went to the clothing shop and picked one _____.

7. Kathryn gave the shoemaker her claim check so that she could pick ___ her shoes that were repaired.

8. Claudia piled ___ traffic tickets, mostly because she drove too fast.

9. Jack put two pizzas _____; now he's sick.

10. The government put ___ a new bridge over the river.

11. We were really put ____ by how dirty the restaurant was.

12. The bartender put the two boys ____ of the pub for being under age.

13. We put ___ some files that added two more pages to our website.

14. We put ____ ____ the noise from the construction for a week.

15. Hair and other things plugged ___ the shower drain.

16. I caught my boyfriend playing _____ with my best friend.

17. We plan ___ going to China next summer.

18. We knew the company was going to lay us ___; we planned ___ it.

19. The festival organizers planned _____ for the big celebration.

20. Claudia piled the cheese ___ the pizza. It was good.

Chapter 10
*Phrasal verbs beginning with the letter **R***

In this section you will learn how to use many different phrasal verbs beginning with the letter R correctly in a sentence.

There are two kinds of phrasal verbs, separable and inseparable. Separable phrasal verbs can take an object between the verb and the preposition. For example: *My father <u>picked</u> me <u>up</u> after school and drove me home.* Inseparable phrasal verbs cannot take an object between the verb and the preposition. For example: I asked my friends to <u>*come along*</u> with me to the Christmas party. <u>*Come along*</u> cannot be separated by an object.

The numbers in front of the examples that are in parenthesis (), correspond the to number of the explanation found directly above. So, for example: 1. *explanation* . . . refers to (1) *example* . . . . If there is only one explanation or meaning given for the phrasal verb, then there will be two examples given for the one explanation. Both examples will be marked with (1).

If you have the accompanying Focus on English mp3 audio book (available separately from the school store or from www.FOEBooks.com) listen to each of the phrasal verbs, followed by their meanings and then some examples of how they are used in real English sentences. Each example will be spoken twice. There will be a review at the end of this chapter.

There will be a review at the end of this chapter.

Phrasal verbs beginning with the letter R

Read and / or listen carefully to the examples, as they will give you a good idea as to how to use the phrasal verb in real English sentences.

Rip off *(separable):* 1. To tear or pull away, sometimes violently, as in this example: *Chama **ripped** the top **off** of the flour box and poured the flour into a bowl.* 2. *(informal)* To steal or take something without authorization from its owner (recently: means to download music files from the Internet, sometimes without complete authorization from the owners of the music), as in this example: *My bicycle was **ripped off** yesterday and I had to walk home from school.*

    More examples:
- (1) The check-in clerk at the airport *ripped* the old tags *off* of my luggage and put new ones on.
- (2) Somebody *ripped off* my jacket from the back of my chair.

Rip up *(separable):* 1. To tear paper or cardboard, as in this example: *Alex **ripped up** the traffic ticket and said he wasn't going to pay the fine.*

    More examples:
- (1) The clerk *ripped up* the cardboard box into small pieces and then threw it away.

- (1) The worker *ripped up* the old clothing and used it for rags.

Rule out (separable): 1. To exclude from consideration, to exclude as a possibility, as in this example: *We **ruled out** going to Majorca this year because it was too expensive.*

More examples:
- (1) The teacher *ruled out* giving extra homework because it was a holiday.
- (1) Tim *ruled out* going to his friend's house because it was too late at night.

Run across (inseparable): 1. To encounter or meet, usually unexpectedly, as in this example: *I **ran across** my classmate from school while I was shopping at the mall.*

More examples:
- (1) Patrick *ran across* a problem while doing his homework.
- (1) Megumi *ran across* a diamond earring lying in the sand while walking at the beach.

Run around (inseparable): 1. To hurriedly go here and there, as in this example: *Just before the party, I **ran around** looking for a new jacket at some of the clothing stores in town.*

More examples:
- (1) Right before the exam I *ran around* asking people to lend me a pencil.
- (1) Mattias *ran around* the beach asking people if they knew what time it was.

Run down *(separable):* 1. Can mean to find or locate something that you were looking for, as in this example: *I finally **ran down** that diamond necklace I was looking for.* 2. To hit with a vehicle, as in this example: *The woman was hurt badly when the car **ran** her **down**.* 3. To chase and catch someone or something, as in this example: *The police **ran** the criminal **down** and put him back in jail.*

More examples:
- (1) I finally ***ran down*** that computer software I was looking for.
- (2) In the early morning, the milk truck accidentally ***ran down*** the dog that was lying in the street.
- (3) The crowd ***ran down*** the purse snatcher and held him until the police arrived.

Run into *(separable):* 1. Can mean to meet or encounter unexpectedly; similar, but not identical in meaning to ***run across***, as in this example: *I **ran into** my best friend while I was shopping in town.* 2. To hit or collide with something, as in this example: *The car **ran into** the telephone pole because the driver was drunk.* 3. To amount to or to be approximately valued at, as in this example: *The owner's net worth **runs into** the millions of dollars.* (Note: *we often use a noun phrase after using the expression run into with this meaning.*)

More examples:
- (1) Toshiko ***ran into*** an old friend while walking downtown.

Page 158

- (2) The drunken man *ran into* the door while leaving the pub.
- (3) The cost of rebuilding the city after the storm will *run into* the millions of dollars.

Run out *(separable):* 1. To exhaust, to deplete, to have no more of something, to be out of something, as in this example: *My car **ran out** of gas on the way to work.* 2. To leave unexpectedly; sometimes used in a negative context to mean permanently, as in this example: *My wife **ran out** on me, and now I am all alone.* 3. To put out by force, to force someone to leave, as in this example: *The townspeople **ran** the thief **out** of town.*

More examples:
- (1) I couldn't complete the race because I *ran out* of energy.
- (2) Jim's partner *ran out* on him and took all of his money.
- (3) The bartender *ran* the troublemaker *out* of the pub.

Run over *(separable):* 1. To collide with, knock down, and often pass over, as in this example: *The car **ran over** the chicken that was crossing the road.* 2. To review something, usually quickly, as in this example: *The politician **ran over** his speech before going on stage.* 3. To exceed a limit, usually used with time, as in this example: *We had to pay extra because we **ran over** our time limit.*

More examples:
- (1) The car *ran over* a nail in the road and got a flat tire.

- (2) The student *ran over* his presentation before giving it to the class.
- (3) The policeman gave us a parking ticket because we *ran over* our time.

Run up (separable): 1. To accumulate a tab or bill, as in this example: *We ran up a big bill at the bar and the bartender asked us to pay before we have any more drinks.* 2. To run to a higher level, as in this example: *Jack and Jill ran up the hill.* 3. To approach someone or something quickly, as in this example: *The concert fan ran up to the rock star and asked for an autograph.*

More examples:
- (1) We really *ran up* a big bill when we went shopping today.
- (2) The marathon runners *ran up* the steep hill.
- (3) My son *ran up* to me and asked me if he could have a new bicycle like his friend has.

Chapter 10 review

Phrasal verbs beginning with the letter **R**

Instructions: read and /or listen carefully to the sentences below. Fill in the blank spaces with the correct **preposition, particle,** *or* **adverb***. The answers can be found in this chapter (above).*

1. Mattias ran _____ the beach asking people if they knew what time it was.

2. We really ran ____ a big bill when we went shopping today.

3. The car ran ____ a nail in the road and got a flat tire.

4. Toshiko ran ____ an old friend while walking downtown.

5. I couldn't complete the race because I ran ____ of energy.

6. I finally ran ____ that computer software I was looking for.

7. Patrick ran ____ a problem while doing his homework.

8. Tim ruled ____ going to his friend's house because it was too late at night.

9. The worker ripped ____ the old clothing and used it for rags.

10. Somebody ripped ____ my jacket from the back of my chair.

Chapter 11
Phrasal verbs beginning with the letter **S**

In this section you will learn how to use many different phrasal verbs beginning with the letter S correctly in a sentence.

There are two kinds of phrasal verbs, separable and inseparable. Separable phrasal verbs can take an object between the verb and the preposition. For example: *My father <u>picked</u> me <u>up</u> after school and drove me home.* Inseparable phrasal verbs cannot take an object between the verb and the preposition. For example: I asked my friends to <u>come along</u> with me to the Christmas party. <u>Come along</u> cannot be separated by an object.

The numbers in front of the examples that are in parenthesis (), correspond the to number of the explanation found directly above. So, for example: 1. *explanation . . .* refers to (1) *example . . . .* If there is only one explanation or meaning given for the phrasal verb, then there will be two examples given for the one explanation. Both examples will be marked with (1).

If you have the accompanying Focus on English mp3 audio book (available separately from the school store or from www.FOEBooks.com) listen to each of the phrasal verbs, followed by their meanings and then some examples of how they are used in real English sentences. Each example will be spoken twice. There will be a review at the end of this chapter.

Page 162

There will be a review at the end of this chapter.

Phrasal verbs beginning with the letter S

Read and / or listen carefully to the examples, as they will give you a good idea as to how to use the phrasal verb in real English sentences.

Screw on(to) *(separable):* 1. To fasten something to something else using screws, as in this example: *We screwed the bulletin board on(to) the wall.* 2. To tighten a top on a jar or other container with a screw top, as in this example: *After removing the beans from the jar, Sophie **screwed** the top back **on**.* (Note: We use the word "back" in English a lot, usually with the meaning "return.")

More examples:
- (1) We **screwed** the part **on**(to) the car motor and then started up the motor.
- (2) Mark unscrewed the top from the sugar jar, got one tablespoon of sugar, and then **screwed** the top back **on**.

Screw out of *(separable):* 1. *(informal)* To cheat or defraud someone out of something, as in this example: *The ticket seller sold us invalid tickets; we got **screwed out of** $20 each.*

More examples:
- (1) The investors were **screwed out of** millions of dollars because the stocks they bought had no value.

- (1) My brother counted the change that the vendor returned to us and discovered that the vendor tried to *screw* us *out of* $5.

Screw up *(separable):* 1. *(informal)* To make a mistake or miscalculation, as in this example: *The vendor **screwed up** and gave us the wrong change.* 2. *(informal)* Is also used to mean contort or change a facial expression, as in this example: *When I told the vendor that he had made a mistake and had given me the wrong change, the vendor **screwed up** his face and then gave me the correct change.* 3. *(informal)* Another meaning is to injure, as in this example: *My friend **screwed up** his ankle while skiing.*

More examples:
- (1) I ***screwed up*** and got a bad grade on the exam.
- (2) The teacher ***screwed up*** his face and then gave the student the bad news about his exam results.
- (3) I ***screwed up*** my thumb trying to stop a soccer goal from getting into the goal.

See about *(inseparable):* 1. English speakers will use the word see to mean *talk to in person*, as in this example: *The teachers said that he wanted to **see** me **about** my exam grade.* 2. Can also be used to refer to the future, when someone is interested in experiencing the results of something that is or has been said, or that is happening or has happened in the near past, as in this example: *My brother said he was going to be a better person in the future. I told him that we would have to wait and **see about** that.*

More examples:
- (1) I went to ***see*** my doctor ***about*** my sore arm.

- (2) My classmate said that I would probably not get a good grade on the exam. I told her that we would *see about* that.

Sell out (separable): 1. To sell all of something that you had to sell, as in this example: *The price of apples was cheap and people came and bought all his apples. He was **sold out** in about two hours.* 2. To betray someone, especially when the betrayer was someone you trusted; to betray an idea or principle, as in this example: *During the war we were safely hidden in the mountains until someone we knew and trusted **sold** us **out** to the enemy. The enemy then found our hiding place, captured us, and then put us in jail.*

  More examples:
  - (1) Excuse me, do you have any mp3 players left? I am sorry, but we are all *sold out* of that item.
  - (2) My classmates *sold* me *out* and told the teacher I didn't hand in the homework assignment.

Set out (inseparable): 1. To embark on or undertake; to begin a journey, venture, or project; to have the intention to do something, as in this example: *The explorer **set out** to find the lost continent of Atlantis.* 2. To carefully and systematically lay out plans, rules or ideas, as in this example: *My girlfriend and I entered a cooking contest. Before the contest began, the judge **set out** the rules of the competition so that everyone was clear about them.*

  More examples:
  - (1) In 1492 Columbus *set out* to find a shorter route to India.

Page 165

- (2) The coach of our soccer team *set out* plans for playing our competition today.

Set up (separable): 1. To assemble, build or erect something, as in this example: *The mechanics set up the new machine.* 2. To establish someone with authority or power, as in this example: *After the war, the military set up the dictator.* 3. (informal) To be tricked or deceived into doing something that could be dangerous, as in this example: *The gangsters set him up to do something illegal. The police will probably catch him and he will go to jail.*

More examples:
- (1) The students *set up* a table at the science fair.
- (2) Powerful and wealthy businessmen *set* their representative *up* to lead the country.
- (3) His friends *set* him *up* to meet the girl. They convinced him that the girl liked him and wanted to meet him. Really, they knew that the girl had no interest in him and they knew that the girl would get mad at him if he spoke to her.

Settle down (separable): 1. To begin living a more stable life, a more settled life, as in this example: *Jim thought that it was time for him to settle down and make a nice life for himself, so he asked his girlfriend to marry him.* 2. To calm down, to become less nervous or restless, as in this example: *Silvia was really upset about the traffic accident that she witnessed. Her mother finally talked to her and helped her to settle down a little.*

More examples:

Page 166

- (1) The salesman traveled from city to city for his job, but dreamed about the day when he could *settle down* in one location.
- (2) Gina's purse was stolen. She was so upset she couldn't describe the thief to the police. Finally, the police asked her to *settle down*, relax and have a cup of water.

Settle for *(inseparable):* 1. To accept what is offered, even though it is not what you really want; To accept less than what was expected, as in this example: *Rita advertised her car for $5000, but she **settled for** $4500 when a buyer made the offer.*

More examples:
- (1) The house was up for sale for $100,000, but the owner told the salesman to *settle for* a little less money to make a fast sale.
- (1) Mika was hoping to get a perfect score on the exam, but she had to *settle for* 98% because of a small error she made.

Shake off *(separable):* 1. To get rid of something; to free yourself of something, as in this example: *The dog came in from the rain and **shook** himself **off**. He made everything we around him!* 2. To deliberately ignore bad feelings or pain and, usually, continue doing what you were doing, as in this example: *The runner fell at the beginning of the competition but he **shook** it **off**, got up and continued racing.*

More examples:

Page 167

- (1) After two hours of hiking we arrived back at our cabin, *shook* the mud *off* of our shoes and then took them off.
- (2) Marta felt a little sick when she began the exam, but she *shook* it *off* and worked hard to get a good grade.

Shake up (separable): 1. To vigorously mix, as in this example: *I combined some oil and vinegar with some other ingredients, shook them up and made a nice salad dressing.* 2. The result of being badly frightened or emotionally upset by something or someone, as in this example: *The race car driver was shaken up by the accident.* 3. To drastically reorganize or rearrange something, as in this example: *Company sales were down and the president shook up the management. Some managers lost their jobs and other managers had to take a different position.*

More examples:
- (1) After putting the ingredients into the jar, Sarah put the lid on and *shook* them *up*.
- (2) The businessman was *shaken up* by the sudden downturn in the economy.
- (3) The voters in the country *shook up* the government with a new leadership and many new faces. (Note: We use the word "faces" in English to mean people; "new faces" to mean who have never been in a certain position before.)

Show off (separable): 1. To act or behave in a way that deliberately tries to bring the attention of others to yourself, as in this example: *The boy was riding his bicycle on only one wheel and **showing off** to all the people that were watching.*

More examples:
- (1) Jean wanted to **show off** her new clothes at the school party.
- (2) Yolanda likes to **show off** by riding her skateboard around town.

Show up *(separable):* 1. To arrive somewhere, sometimes unexpectedly, or at an unexpected time, as in this example: *We had a birthday party for my aunt but she **showed up** late.* 2. To do better than someone or something else, to surpass, as in this example: *We **showed up** the competition by beating them 5 to 1.* 3. When something can be easily or clearly seen, as in this example: *When you've had too much alcohol to drink, alcohol **shows up** in the blood during a test. If too much alcohol shows up in your blood, the police will not allow you to drive your car.*

More examples:
- (1) The police **showed up** just in time. The mugger tried to run away but the police caught him.
- (2) The new student **showed up** the class by getting the highest mark on the exam.
- (3) When some professional athletes are tested, illegal drugs **show up** in their blood and they are punished for violations.

Shut off *(separable):* 1. To stop the flow of or passage of something, as in this example: *The cook filled the pot with water and then **shut off** the faucet.* 2. To close off, or to block access or

Page 169

block passage, as in this example: *Access to the street was **shut off** due to construction.*

More examples:
- (1) The damage from the storm **shut off** the electricity.
- (2) The entrance to the building was **shut off** to the public because of a police investigation.

Shut up *(separable and inseparable depending on usage)*: 1. *(inseparable)* To stop talking, as in this example: *I told my sister to **shut up** when she said bad things about my boyfriend.* 2. *(separable)* To cause to stop talking, as in this example: *We didn't believe that she was a good student, but her high exam grade really **shut** us **up**.*

More examples:
- (1) The boy tried to explain why he as late but his father told him to **shut up**.
- (2) My boss tried to **shut** me **up** when I told him that his information was incorrect.

Sign in *(separable)*: 1. To record your entrance by writing your name down on a piece of paper or by typing in a user ID or password (or both), as in this example: *Everyone was required to **sign in** before entering the exam room.*

More examples:
- (1) All guests were required to **sign in** at the check-in desk.
- (1) I asked my friend to **sign** me **in**(to) the forum with his password and username.

Sign out *(separable):* 1. To record you exit or departure from a formal meeting, a workplace or location by writing your name on a piece of paper, as in this example: *After the meeting, everyone was required to **sign out** before leaving.* 2. To register the removal of something like a book or merchandise, from a location, as in this example: *I **signed out** two really interesting books from the library.* 3. Sometimes used in radio communications when the speaker informs the listener that he or she will no longer be talking, as in this example: *This is Ai Tanaka **signing out** until our broadcast next week at this time.*
  More examples:
  - (1) After using the employment services computer, you are required to ***sign out*** before leaving.
  - (2) My sister ***signed out*** two library books about gardening.
  - (3) The radio announcer ***signed out*** long after I went to sleep.

Sign up *(separable):* 1. To agree to participate, or receive something by signing your name, as in this example: *I **signed up** for a two-week free trial of the gym membership.*
  More examples:
  - (1) My brother ***signed up*** to join the Army.
  - (1) Sarah ***signed up*** for the two week vacation in Trinidad.

Sit down *(separable or inseparable depending on usage):* 1. *(inseparable)* To take a seat or to change your position to one of sitting, as in this example: *The students **sat down** when the teacher entered the room.* 2. *(separable)* To cause to be in a sitting position, usually when one person needs information from or needs to give advice or admonishment to another, as in this example: *The teacher **sat** the student **down** and gave him the bad news about his low grade on the exam.*

    More examples:
- (1) I got on the bus and ***sat down***.
- (2) The detective ***sat*** the criminal ***down*** and began to ask him some questions.

Slip up *(inseparable):* 1. To make a mistake or error; the feeling of this expression is "accidental," as in this example: *I **slipped up** and got four wrong on the exam.*

    More examples:
- (1) When you are mountain climbing, you cannot afford to ***slip up***.
- (1) I ***slipped up*** and told my brother about the ending to the movie before he had a chance to see it.

Slow down *(separable):* 1. To move more slowly, to cause to move more slowly," as in this example: *We **slowed** the car **down** when we arrived in the city.*

    More examples:
- (1) The policeman ***slowed*** the traffic ***down*** around the accident.
- (1) I have been running around all day and now I just want to ***slow down*** and take a rest.

Sneak in(to) *(inseparable or separable depending on usage):* 1. *(inseparable)* To enter a building, event, or restricted area without being seen or heard, as in this example: *Every Saturday night the kids would **sneak into** the dance party held at the beach club.* 2. *(separable)* To cause something or someone to enter someplace without the knowledge of those in authority, as in this example: *Two of the boys **sneaked** some alcohol **into** the party.*

More examples:
- (1) The student was ten minutes late for class so he tried to ***sneak into*** class when the teacher's back was turned.
- (2) The man tried to ***sneak*** the package ***into*** the airplane but was caught by the stewardess.

Sneak out *(separable or inseparable depending on usage):* 1. *(inseparable)* To leave a building, event, or restricted area without being seen or heard, as in this example: *Some of the boys sat near the door because they wanted to **sneak out** of class early.* 2. *(separable)* To cause something or someone to exit or depart someplace without the knowledge of those in authority, as in this example: *The refugees **sneaked** their families **out** of the country.*

More examples:
- (1) The girl tried to ***sneak out*** of the restaurant without paying her bill.
- (2) The man tried to ***sneak*** the drugs ***out*** of the country but was caught during the security check at the airport.

Sort out *(separable):* 1. To solve or to try to understand a problem or difficulty, as in this example: *The teacher stopped the argument between the two students and tried to **sort out** what the problem was.* 2. To organize or separate things out into smaller, manageable groups, as in this example: *Before washing the clothes, my mother **sorted** them **out** according to color.*

> **More examples:**
> - (1) The customer was arguing with the store clerk, so the store manager came over to ***sort out*** the problem.
> - (2) We had over 20 packages to mail, so we ***sorted*** them ***out*** according to destination and brought them to the post office.

Space out *(separable):* 1. To separate things or people so as to be more or less equal distance from each other, as in this example: *When I came home from shopping, I **spaced** everything I bought **out** on the table.* 2. *(slang or informal)* To lose your focus or train of thought, to be confused about or forget something, as in this example: *While driving to work, I **spaced out** and turned down the wrong street.*

> **More examples:**
> - (1) I brought the mail into the house and ***spaced*** it ***out*** on the table so I could have a look at it.
> - (2) Oh, I totally ***spaced out*** and forgot to invite my best friend to the party.

Stand around *(inseparable):* 1. To stand here or there without purpose, without getting anything done; sometimes used when expressing frustration with workers not getting any work done, as in this example: *We have a lot of work to do and you guys are just **standing around**.*

> **More examples:**
> - (1) I wasn't sure about what I was supposed to do, so I **stood around** for most of the day.
> - (1) We just **stood around** waiting for our friends to arrive.

Stand for *(inseparable):* 1. To tolerate or put up with, as in this example: *One thing that my teacher won't **stand for** is his students not doing their homework.* 2. To represent or to symbolize, as in this example: *The flag of your country **stands for** the unity of the people of your country.*

> **More examples:**
> - (1) The people in our neighborhood won't **stand for** a lot of noise.
> - (2) The symbol or the eagle on my company ID card **stands for** my company.

Stand up *(inseparable or separable, depending on usage):* 1. *(inseparable)* To remain true or valid, sound or durable, as in this example: *The car looks good but it will not **stand up** to hard driving.* 2. *(separable)* To position yourself or something in an upright, standing, vertical position, as in this example: *The hunter **stood** his rifle **up** in the corner or his cabin.* 3. To speak out for, to fight for, or to defend something or someone, as in this example: *I **stood up** for my sister when she was accused of stealing because she is not a thief.*

> **More examples:**

Page 175

- ❑ (1) The book was old and falling apart. It didn't ***stand up*** well to repeated use.
- ❑ (2) I ***stood*** the package ***up*** in the corner while I removed the wrapping.
- ❑ (3) It is important for a person to ***stand up*** for his or her rights.

Start off (inseparable): 1. Expresses: *the beginning* or *in the beginning*; to begin, as in this example: *We **started off** dinner with a nice salad.*
   More examples:
   - ❑ (1) My sister was in a bad mood, she ***started off*** the day by being late for school.
   - ❑ (1) The celebration ***started off*** very nicely, but it soon rained and everyone had to find shelter.

Start out (inseparable): 1. Expresses "the beginning" or "in the beginning" usually as it relates to an action, event, or activity of some kind; we tend to use start out when we are talking about the beginning of an activity that was planned or when we are telling a store about what happened during an activity in the past, as in this example: *We **started out** by going to the Vatican when we were in Rome, but did not have time to see everything in Vatican City.*
   More examples:
   - ❑ (1) When you don't have experience with a new job, you usually ***start out*** by doing small, easy jobs until you have more knowledge.

❏ (1) Most employees *start out* at a low salary and then gradually make more money as they become more experienced.

Start over (separable): 1. To begin again; to do something over, to do something again after already having done it, as in this example: *After the great earthquake destroyed our business, we had to start over again.*
More examples:
❏ (1) The student asked the teacher if he could *start* the exam *over* because there was too much noise outside the classroom and he couldn't concentrate.
❏ (1) I couldn't understand what the girl was saying so I asked her to *start over* and speak more slowly.

Start up (separable): 1. To initiate something, usually a business, club, organization, or other formal group, as in this example: *After finishing school he started up a new business.* 2. To initiate the operation of a mechanical or electrical motor or computer, as in this example: *She started up the car engine and drove to the food market.*
More examples:
❏ (1) We *started up* a new club for English students.
❏ (2) I pushed the button and *started up* the computer.

Stay off (inseparable): 1. Many times used in demands or commands, *stay off* means to not step on, climb on or generally be on something else or on a restricted area, as in this example: *Please stay off the grass!* 2. To keep a distance from, as in this

Page 177

example: *Let's not talk about the negative things about our vacation; let's **stay off** that subject.*

> **More examples:**
> - (1) Please **stay off** the new bicycle until we have made all of the adjustments.
> - (2) When we meet our friends tonight, let's not talk about work; let's **stay off** that subject.

Stay out *(inseparable):* 1. To **stay out** of something means to distance yourself from something, to not get involved with something, often referring to a tricky or difficult problem or something involving other people besides yourself, as in this example: *My sister told me to **stay out** of her personal affairs; she said she could solve her own problems.* 2. To remain away from, usually, home or work, as in this example: *I asked my mother if I could **stay out** until 4am in the morning.*

> **More examples:**
> - (1) My father warned me that it was always best to **stay out** of other people's affairs.
> - (2) What a great party! We **stayed out** all night.

Stay up *(inseparable):* 1. To remain awake beyond the time when you would normally go to bed, as in this example: *My sister and I **stayed up** to see the special program on TV.* 2. To remain at a certain elevation; to remain at a certain high position, as in this example: *With the strong winds, the kite **stayed up** for two hours.*

> **More examples:**

- (1) My family ***stayed up*** for the fourth of July all-night celebration.
- (2) The house was very old and rotted. We didn't know how long it would ***stay up***.

Step on *(inseparable):* 1. To walk or tread on, as in this example: *Be careful not to **step on** any glass with your bare feet.* 2. Can also be used, as in a command, to mean to hurry up, go faster, or to increase speed, as in this example: *Come on, **step on** it! We have to hurry up and get ready if we want to arrive at the theater on time.*

More examples:
- (1) Be careful not to ***step on*** the cat's tail!
- (2) We are going to have to ***step on*** it if we are going to arrive at school in time for the exam.

Stick around *(inseparable):* 1. To remain somewhere longer than expected, as in this example: *After school was over, we **stuck around** for another hour.*

More examples:
- (1) Hey, ***stick around***; don't go home yet! We are going to have some coffee in about ten minutes.
- (1) We ***stuck around*** after work because we wanted to finish our project.

Stick out *(inseparable):* 1. To be obvious, to be prominent; something sticks out when it is more obvious than other things, as in this example: *His red pants really **stuck out**.* 2. Can also be used to express enduring something, or being patient with usually a long process, as in this example: *The show was so boring, but we **stuck** it **out** until the end.*

More examples:
- (1) I had wonderful memories of my vacation to Asia, but the memory that ***stuck out*** was of all of the beautiful temples.
- (2) Work was boring today. After 3pm there was nothing to do; we had to ***stick*** it ***out*** until 5pm.

Stick to (*separable*): 1. To continue doing, believing, or behaving in a certain way; ***stick to*** has the feeling of "not changing" or steadfastness, as in this example: *Even though his friend's idea sounded better, he decided to **stick to** his idea and do it his way.* 2. To remain attached to something, as in this example: *It just finished raining and mud was **sticking to** both sides of the car.* 3. To focus, to remain on subject, as in this example: *It is important for a writer to **stick to** the subject he is writing about and not distract the reader with other information.*

More examples:
- (1) If you feel you are right, then you must ***stick to*** your way of doing things.
- (2) I ***stuck*** the announcement ***to*** the bulletin board with a thumb tack.
- (3) The teacher told the students to ***stick to*** the subject in their essay and not write about things that had nothing to do with the topic.

Stick up (*separable*): 1. To post or put up something for everyone to see, as in this example: *She **stuck** the notice **up** on* *the bulletin board.* 2. To rob, usually with a weapon, as in this example: *The robbers **stuck up** a bank and stole $2 million.* 3. To protrude or to be above a surface, as in this example: *Be careful not to step on the nails **sticking up** from the boards on the floor.*

More examples:
- (1) The teacher **stuck** the students' finished homework assignments **up** on the wall for everyone to see.
- (2) The robber **stuck up** the tourist and took his wallet.
- (3) We just removed the carpet in the living room. Be careful walking in that room because there are still some nails **sticking up** out of the floor.

Stick with *(separable and inseparable depending on usage):* 1. *(inseparable)* To stick with something is to continue to do something the way you have always done it, as in this example: *My sister still **sticks with** her old way of making lamb curry, even though it is easier to make it my way.* 2. *(inseparable)* To continue to use something that you have been using, as in this example: *I'm not getting a new cellular phone. I'm going to **stick with** my old cellular phone because it is more reliable.* 3. *(inseparable)* To remain close to other people, as in this example: *It's really crowded here at the theater. **Stick with** me and I'll find our seats.* 4. *(separable)* To put someone in a position where they have to do something or endure something, as in this example: *I apologized to my colleague for **sticking** him **with** all the work. I had to go home early because of an emergency.*

More examples:

- (1) The people of that country have **_stuck with_** their traditions for hundreds of years.
- (2) I don't like a wireless mouse for my computer. I'm going to **_stick with_** the old style mouse with the wire attached.
- (3) The three orphans **_stuck with_** each other during their childhood.
- (4) The boss **_stuck_** the new employee **_with_** a big project.

Stop off (inseparable): 1. As you travel to a destination you stop briefly to visit with or do something, as in this example: *On my way home, I **stopped off** at the grocery store to buy some eggs.*

More examples:
- (1) On my way to the supermarket I **_stopped off_** at my friend's house for a brief conversation.
- (1) On my way to school, I **_stopped off_** at the convenience store to buy some coffee.

Stop over (inseparable): 1. As you travel to a destination, usually by plane, you stop briefly, and then continue on your way, as in this example: *On our way to Europe, we **stopped over** in Chicago for one night.*

More examples:
- (1) On our way to Asia, we **_stopped over_** in Hawaii for a couple of days.
- (1) The plane **_stopped over_** in New York to make some repairs to the engine.

Straighten out *(separable):* 1. To correct, to make correct, as in this example: *We had a problem with our airline ticket reservations but the clerk **straightened** it **out**.* 2. To make straight; to mechanically change a curved or crooked item so that it is straight, as in this example: *My car antenna was bent, so I **straightened** it **out**.* 3. *(informal)* To straighten someone out is to do or say something to someone that causes them to change their behavior or to understand something better, as in this example: *One of the students was acting foolishly so the teacher went over, said something to him, and **straightened** him **out**.*

More examples:
- (1) There was a misunderstanding about the homework assignment, but the teacher **straightened** us **out** about it.
- (2) Marcus **straightened out** his rear bicycle wheel by tightening up some of the spokes.
- (3) One of the students was throwing paper at another student until the teacher came over and **straightened** him **out** about his behavior.

Straighten up *(separable):* 1. To clean up or organize something, as in this example: *My mother told me to **straighten up** my room.* 2. To change something that is bent or crooked to being straight, as in this example: *Your drawing is good but some of the lines are crooked. Please **straighten up** your lines.*

More examples:
- (1) Before we can have a party, we have to **straighten up** our apartment.

- (2) Students, please sit straight in your chairs. Do not curve or hunch your backs, please. Please **_straighten up_** in your seats.

Stress out *(separable):* 1. *(informal)* To be worried, anxious or nervous about something, as in this example: *I was really **stressed out** about adopting a child from the orphanage.*
> **More examples:**
> - (1) The students were **_stressed out_** about taking the important exam.
> - (1) Some of the members of our soccer team were really **_stressed out_** about the upcoming game.

Switch off *(separable):* 1. To stop the power to something, to turn off, to stop the operation of something, as in this example: *When we left the classroom, we **switched off** the lights.*
> **More examples:**
> - (1) After cutting the grass, Toshiko **_switched off_** the lawn mower and put it back in the garage.
> - (1) When you are finished using the computer, please **_switch_** it **_off_**. Thank you.

Switch on *(separable):* 1. To allow power to energize something, to turn something on, to begin the operation of something, as in this example: *Upon entering the classroom, we **switched on** the lights.*
> **More examples:**
> - (1) Jean went into the computer room and **_switched on_** the computer.

❏ (1) Please put the dishes in the dishwasher and then *switch* it *on*.

Chapter 11 review

Phrasal verbs beginning with the letter S

Instructions: *read and /or listen carefully to the sentences below. Fill in the blank spaces with the correct* **preposition, particle,** *or* **adverb***. The answers can be found in this chapter (above).*

1. We screwed the part _____ the car motor and then started _____ the motor.

2. I screwed _____ and got a bad grade on the exam.

3. I went to see my doctor _____ my sore arm.

4. After cutting the grass, Toshiko switched _____ the lawn mower and put it back in the garage.

5. The students were stressed _____ about taking the important exam.

6. Before we can have a party, we have to straighten _____ our apartment.

7. Marcus straightened _____ his rear bicycle wheel by tightening up some of the spokes.

8. My classmates sold me _____ and told the teacher I didn't hand in the homework assignment.

9. The students set ___ a table at the science fair.

10. In 1492 Columbus set ___ to find a shorter route to India.

11. The salesman traveled from city to city for his job, but dreamed about the day when he could settle _____ in one location.

12. The boy tried to explain why he as late but his father told him to shut ____.

13. All guests were required to sign ___ at the check-in desk.

14. I have been running around all day and now I just want to slow _____ and take a rest.

15. The man tried to sneak the package _____ the airplane but was caught by the stewardess.

16. The customer was arguing with the store clerk, so the store manager came over to sort ____ the problem.

17. I brought the mail into the house and spaced it _____ on the table so I could have a look at it.

18. We just stood _____ waiting for our friends to arrive.

19. It is important for a person to stand ____ for his or her rights.

20. My sister was in a bad mood, she started ____ the day by being late for school.

Chapter 12
Phrasal verbs beginning with the letter T

In this section you will learn how to use many different phrasal verbs beginning with the letter T correctly in a sentence.

There are two kinds of phrasal verbs, separable and inseparable. Separable phrasal verbs can take an object between the verb and the preposition. For example: *My father **picked** me **up** after school and drove me home.* Inseparable phrasal verbs cannot take an object between the verb and the preposition. For example: I asked my friends to **come along** with me to the Christmas party. **Come along** cannot be separated by an object.

The numbers in front of the examples that are in parenthesis (), correspond the to number of the explanation found directly above. So, for example: 1. *explanation . . .* refers to (1) *example . . . .* If there is only one explanation or meaning given for the phrasal verb, then there will be two examples given for the one explanation. Both examples will be marked with (1).

If you have the accompanying Focus on English mp3 audio book (available separately from the school store or from www.FOEBooks.com) listen to each of the phrasal verbs, followed by their meanings and then some examples of how they are used in real English sentences. Each example will be spoken twice. There will be a review at the end of this chapter.

Page 187

There will be a review at the end of this chapter.

Phrasal verbs beginning with the letter T

Read and / or listen carefully to the examples, as they will give you a good idea as to how to use the phrasal verb in real English sentences.

Take apart *(separable):* 1. To disassemble, to separate into pieces, as in this example: *The workman **took** the washing machine **apart** so that he could repair it.* 2. To dissect for the purpose of analyzing something; to analyze something, as in this example: *The committee took the idea apart to see if there were any problems with it.* (Here, take apart, means "analyze.")
> **More examples:**
> - (1) My alarm clock stopped working so I **took** it **apart** to see if I could repair it.
> - (2) Our class project was about the idea of freedom. Our group had to **take apart** the idea of freedom and then make a presentation about this topic to the class.

Take in *(separable):* 1. To accept or receive someone or something as a guest, employee, or an adopted member of the family, as in this example: *My parents **took in** a little boy who lost his parents.* 2. To diminish in size or make smaller; to decrease the size of something, a diameter or overall width, as in this example: *The seamstress **took in** the girl's dress.* (Note:

A seamstress is a person who sews clothing, makes changes to clothing, or makes new clothing.) 3. To include as part of something else, as in this example: *The exam **takes in** all of the irregular past tense English verbs.* 4. To deceive, cheat, swindle, defraud someone, as in this example: *The old people were **taken in** by a con artist. They lost all of their money.* 5. To look at or view thoroughly, to look and to take the time to understand what you are looking at; sometimes used to express a sightseeing excursion, as in this example: *Last year we went to Rome and **took in** the sights.*

More examples:
- (1) Last week, Myoung Hoon ***took in*** a stray cat and gave it a new home.
- (2) The tailor ***took in*** the man's pants so that they would fit better. (Meaning: A tailor is a man who sews clothing. A seamstress is a woman who sews clothing. Sometimes clothing is too big for a person, so a tailor or seamstress will change the size of the clothing by making it smaller in places, by taking it in, so that the clothing will feel more comfortable to the person who wears it.)
- (3) The new immigration form ***takes in*** all of the applicant's background information.
- (4) My friend Blake discovered that the tickets that he bought for the big soccer match were no good. A swindler ***had taken*** him ***in***. (Meaning: a swindler is a person who deceives others, often taking money from people but giving nothing of value back.)

- (5) As I walked into the new building, I slowly *took in* everything that I saw.

Take off (separable): 1. To remove something from something or someone, as in this example: *The woman **took off** her jacket and put it on the chair.* 2. To give a discount, to deduct some money from a price, as in this example: *Janice bought a dress at the mall. The store **took** 20% **off** the regular price.* 3. (slang) To go off in a hurry, as in this example: *Stefan really **took off** when he realized that he was late for class.* 4. Used to talk about a plane leaving the ground, as in this example: *The plane **took off** for Hawaii at 6pm.* 5. To withdraw or discontinue something, as in this example: *The restaurant **took** the tomato soup **off** the menu.* 6. To become very popular, usually a book, movie or music, as in this example: *The movie really **took off**. On the very first day, the movie earned 75 million dollars.*

More examples:
- (1) The man entered the building and *took off* his raincoat.
- (2) The saleslady *took* 10% *off* of the cost of the clothing because we shop there often.
- (3) When the robber saw the police coming, he really *took off*.
- (4) When the plane *took off*, I knew that our vacation began.
- (5) The school *took* Mark's name *off* of the activities list because he was sick.
- (6) The new magazine became popular quickly; it really *took off*!

Take on *(separable)*: 1. To accept or begin an activity, responsibility, or action, as in this example: *Our group **took on** the responsibility of completing the business project.* 2. To challenge someone or something, as in this example: *Our soccer team **took on** the opposition from across town.* 3. To hire, usually for employment, as in this example: *The company **took on** three new employees.*

More examples:
- (1) The new employee ***took on*** a big workload.
- (2) The Dallas Cowboy football team ***took on*** the Miami Dolphin football team.
- (3) My boss ***took on*** two more employees to help with the project.

Take out *(separable)*: 1. To remove something from something or somewhere, or withdraw something, as in this example: *The doctor took the splinter out of my foot.* 2. To apply for and receive a license, permit, or other formal authorization, as in this example: *In our State, you have to **take out** a license before you can hunt.* 3. To escort, as on a romantic date, as in this example: *I **took** my girlfriend **out** to the movies last night.* 4. To let out or vent your emotional feelings on someone or something, as in this example: *Mary did poorly on the exam. When she got home she **took** her frustration **out on** the dog. The dog had no idea why Mary was yelling at him.*

More examples:
- (1) We ***took*** the fast food ***out*** and ate it at the park.

- (2) In most cities, you have to *take out* a special permit in order to build a house.
- (3) I *took* my wife *out* for our anniversary.
- (4) I couldn't believe that the policeman gave me a ticket. When I got home, I was in a bad mood. I *took* my anger *out on* everyone who talked to me.

Take over (separable): 1. To assume control of, or management of, something, as in this example: *A new manager **took over** our department.*

More examples:
- (1) A new company *took over* the management of the building.
- (1) When mom was on vacation, dad *took over* the care of the children.

Take to (inseparable): 1. To like something, or to become attached to something, as in this example: *The family really **took to** their new home, meeting neighbors and making new friends.* 2. To escape to, seek refuge or seek safety, as in this example: *The flood waters were rising quickly. Everyone had to **take to** the hills.*

More examples:
- (1) Rafael really *took to* his brand new car.
- (2) The military invasion forced the refugees to *take to* safer territory over the border.

Take up (separable): 1. To raise something; to make something higher as with clothing alteration, as in this example: *The* seamstress ***took up*** the hem on Sally's dress because it was too long. 2. To accept a bet or a challenge; usually used with the preposition *on*, as in this example: *I **took** him **up** on his bet that I couldn't finish the marathon.* (Meaning: Someone bet me that I could not finish the marathon. I said that I could. I ***took*** him ***up*** on his bet, meaning I accepted his bet. If I finish the marathon, then he has to pay me money.) 3. To begin again, to resume something, as in this example: *This discussion is very important but we have to go to class now. Let's **take** this **up** later when we have time.* 4. To use up or exhaust something; to use up room or space, as in this example: *We can only fit thirty people in this room. More than that will **take up** too much space.* 5. To develop an interest in something, like a hobby, activity, sport, etc., as in this example: *I **took up** skiing last year and now I really like it.*

More examples:
- (1) The tailor ***took up*** the hem on Jim's new pants.
- (2) Hiro bet me $5.00 I couldn't jump over that fence. I ***took him*** up on his bet.
- (3) Look, it's getting late and we should talk about this more. Let's ***take*** this ***up*** again tomorrow afternoon at the coffee shop.
- (4) I'm sorry, but there is no more sugar. We baked a cake last night and that ***took up*** all the sugar that we had.
- (5) My wife ***took up*** knitting. She is now knitting a new blanket for our bed.

Talk down to *(inseparable):* 1. To talk to someone with insulting, belittling condescension; to let someone know that you think very little of them; at act of superiority, as in this example: *The owner of the large home often **talked down to** his servants.*

> **More examples:**
> - (1) The student who had the highest grade on the exam often **talked down to** the other students.
> - (1) The famous actress would sometimes **talk down to** her fans.

Talk into (separable): 1. To convince someone to do something that they probably didn't want to do, as in this example: *My friend **talked** me **into** going with him to the horror movie. I usually don't watch horror movies.*

> **More examples:**
> - (1) My wife **talked** me **into** going shopping with her.
> - (1) My sister **talked** me **into** helping her wash the dishes.

Talk out of (separable): 1. To convince someone not to do something that sometimes they felt they needed to do, as in this example: *My friend **talked** me **out of** going with him to the horror movie because he wanted to be alone with his girlfriend. I really wanted to see that movie.*

> **More examples:**
> - (1) My boss **talked** me **out of** quitting my job.
> - (1) Sun Wa **talked** her friend, Christina, **out of** spending money on a new car.

Tear down *(separable):* 1. To demolish, raze, or level something to the ground, as in this example: *The construction team **tore down** the building so that they could build a new one.* 2. Sometimes used to mean 'take something apart,' usually a motor, as in this example: *The mechanic **tore down** the engine to see what was wrong with it.*

> **More examples:**
> - (1) Hey, what happened to your house? Oh, they ***tore*** it ***down***. They are going to build a new one starting next week.
> - (2) We ***tore down*** the motorcycle engine and put new parts in it.

Tear off *(separable):* 1. To rip or remove with force, something that is flexible, as in this example: *My brother **tore** the top **off** of the cereal box.* 2. *(informal)* To leave hurriedly, as in this example: *The kids **tore off** when they heard the ice cream truck coming.*

> **More examples:**
> - (1) The workers ***tore*** the ***roof*** off of the house so that they could put a new one on.
> - (2) The orphan stole an apple from the fruit stand and then ***tore off*** into the crowd.

Tear up *(separable):* 1. To rip something up, as paper, cardboard or other flexible material, as in this example: *Walter Lu **tore up** the bill from the water company because he already paid them.* 2. *(informal)* To have a wild party or celebration that ends up damaging the party area, as in this example: *The students* *partied all night long. They had a great time, but they really **tore up** the place.*

> **More examples:**
> - (1) She was so angry about her grades that she ***tore up*** her grades report.
> - (2) The guests had a too much alcohol to drink and the party got very wild. They really ***tore up*** the party room and the pool area.

Tell apart *(separable):* 1. To see the difference between one thing or person and another, to distinguish between, as in this example: *The twins were identical. I couldn't **tell** them **apart**.*

> **More examples:**
> - (1) I don't taste any difference between this drink and that drink. I can't ***tell*** them ***apart***.
> - (1) I can't remember the names of the two cats. They are so similar, I can't ***tell*** them ***apart***.

Think about *(inseparable):* 1. To spend time considering something; to focus on something in your thoughts, as in this example: *After the exam, I thought about the questions that I might have gotten wrong.*

> **More examples:**
> - (1) The salesman wanted to sell me the computer, but I wanted to ***think about*** it first.
> - (1) Before getting married, you need to ***think about*** it. (Meaning: Carefully consider what it means to be married.)

Think ahead *(inseparable):* 1. When thinking about something, think about what might be needed in the future or what the consequences of an action will be in the future or what will happen in the future, as in this example: *When starting a new business, always **think ahead**.*

> **More examples:**
> - (1) When planning a project, ***think ahead***. What will the problems be? What will you need to complete the project?
> - (1) If you ***think ahead***, you will avoid a lot of problems.

Think over *(separable):* 1. To consider carefully, as in this example: *Before I buy this new house, I want to **think** it **over**.*

> **More examples:**
> - (1) Don't quit your job yet. ***Think*** it ***over***, maybe you can find a way to get the things you want at your company.
> - (1) My teacher gave me a choice: take the exam, or stay at the same level for the next term. I have to ***think*** this ***over***.

Throw away *(separable):* 1. To discard something or dispose of something, as in this example: *After opening the present, I **threw away** the gift-wrapping.* 2. To foolishly discard something, as in this example: *He **threw away** his whole life because of his drug habit.*

> **More examples:**

- (1) Bridget _**threw away**_ the old batteries and installed new ones in her MP3 player.
- (2) After he got angry with his boss, he knew he _**threw away**_ his chance at a promotion.

**Throw out** (separable): 1. To discard something or dispose of something that is not needed, as in this example: _After opening the present, I **threw out** the gift-wrapping._ 2. To force someone to leave a place or a position, especially in an abrupt manner, as in this example: _The judge at the tennis match **threw** the player **out** of the game because the player was not following the rules._ 3. Used to talk about the cause of a pain or an injury, usually when doing something physical; when bones in a part of the body are not properly lined up or out of alignment, as in this example: _I **threw** my back **out** yesterday carrying that heavy sofa._ 4. In the sport of baseball, a player puts another player out by touching him with the ball, as in this example: _The First baseman **threw out** the runner._

More examples:
- (1) I opened the package of gum and _**threw out**_ the wrapper.
- (2) The people did not like the new leader and _**threw**_ him _**out**_ of office during the next election.
- (3) The woman _**threw out**_ her back when she lifted the child.
- (4) The pitcher _**threw out**_ the runner on second base.

**Throw up** (separable or inseparable depending on usage): 1. (inseparable) To vomit, as in this example: _After drinking_ whiskey all night, Kelly got sick and **threw up** in the bathroom. 2. (*separable*) To build something very quickly and without care, as in this example: *The house was poorly built; they **threw** it **up** in about a week.*

>   More examples:
>   - (1) Alicia was sick all day. She ***threw up*** twice.
>   - (2) The building was hastily constructed. They ***threw*** it ***up*** in three weeks. We don't think that it is safe.

Track down (*separable*): 1. To find someone or something after searching, as in this example: *We finally **tracked down** the sales report. We couldn't find it for two weeks.*

>   More examples:
>   - (1) The reporter ***tracked*** the politician ***down*** and asked him some questions.
>   - (1) Our company has spent a lot of time ***tracking down*** an electronics engineer.

Trade in (*separable*): 1. Some businesses will accept an older item as partial payment towards a new item purchased from them, as in this example: *When we bought our new car we got a discount because we **traded in** our old car.*

>   More examples:
>   - (1) The computer store allowed me to ***trade in*** my old laptop as partial payment for a new one.
>   - (1) Our school allows us to ***trade in*** our old text books for newer ones. We can save a lot of money on books this way.

Page 199

Trick into (separable): 1. Similar in meaning to con into; to use deceit, or to fool someone into doing something they probably would not have done, as in this example: *The salesman **tricked** me **into** buying a used car that needed repairs.*
- (1) On April fools day I was ***tricked into*** believing that there was no school the next day.
- (1) Be careful of con men, because they will ***trick*** you ***into*** buying things that are worthless.

Try on (separable): 1. To wear a piece of clothing to test it, to see if it fits properly and it looks good on you, as in this example: *My friend **tried on** the new shirt, but it didn't fit and the color was ugly.*

More examples:
- (1) Rita Chen ***tried on*** the new dress and she loved it.
- (1) Mark ***tried on*** the pants but they were too big.

Try out (separable): 1. To use or test something before purchasing it or before committing to it, as in this example: *Alex **tried out** the new skis, but he didn't like them.* 2. When you want to join a competition or team, sometimes you have to demonstrate your abilities in a qualifying test; to demonstrate to qualify for an athletic event or team, as in this example: *Before joining the bicycle club, you have to **try out** by riding 25 miles in just one hour. If you can't do this, you can't join the club.*

More examples:
- (1) Tom ***tried out*** the new surfboard before he purchased it from the store.

- (2) Sue Chan *tried out* for the swimming team and made it. (💡 "Made it" means that she was successful.)

Turn around *(separable):* 1. To reverse your direction, to change your orientation completely, or to look in the opposite direction, as in this example: *Oh no, you drove past the theater!* ***Turn around*** *and go back.* 2. To change the condition of something or a situation for the positive, as in this example: *Last year we were losing money in our business, but this year we have **turned around** and made a profit.*

   More examples:
   - (1) ***Turn around*** and look who is coming towards us.
   - (2) Our team was losing the game, but in the last five minutes we have completely ***turned around***. Now we are winning.

Turn down *(separable):* 1. To decline or refuse to accept something; usually used when someone makes you an offer, as in this example: *Rodney made me an offer of $10,000 for my car, but I **turned** him **down** because the offer was too low.* 2. To reduce or diminish the speed, volume, intensity or flow of something, as in this example: ***Turn down*** *the volume on that radio, it's too loud!*

   More examples:
   - (1) My friend offered to drive me to the concert, but I ***turned*** him ***down*** because my girlfriend is going to drive me there.

- (2) There is too much water flowing into the swimming pool; please _turn_ the water _down_!

Turn in (separable): 1. To return or hand something back, similar to *hand in*, as in this example: *The students **turned in** their homework.* 2. To alert the authorities, the police or other public agency, about where a criminal is hiding or is located; also used when you have captured a wanted criminal and you deliver the criminal to the police, as in this example: *I spotted the thief going into an apartment so I called the police and **turned** him **in**.*

More examples:
- (1) After I finished filling out the form, I _turned_ it _in_ to the clerk.
- (2) The police are offering a $1,000 reward for the capture of the bandit. If you _turn_ this bandit _in_ you get $1,000!

Turn into (separable): 1. To become, or change into, to change, as in this example: *After the man drank the smoking chemical he **turned into** a monster!*

More examples:
- (1) It was raining this morning, but now it's sunny; boy, it's really _turned into_ a nice day!
- (1) Wow, the construction company did a good job of restoring that old building; they _turned_ it _into_ something very beautiful.

Turn off *(separable):* 1. To stop the operation of something, like a mechanical or electrical device, or stop the flow of something, or to shut off, as in this example: *Before leaving the factory, we **turned off** the machines and then turned off the lights.* 2. To leave, divert off of, or move off of a path, road, or route that you had been traveling, as in this example: *We **turned off** the road at the second stop light and then drove into the driveway.* 3. *(informal)* When something or someone causes you to feel dislike, displeasure, revulsion, or boredom, as in this example: *We were really **turned off** by the movie. It was so boring.*

More examples:
- (1) It's 2 o'clock in the morning, would you please ***turn off*** your television!
- (2) Travel down Main Street until you get to 5th Avenue, then ***turn off*** at 5th Avenue and travel for 5 miles. The library is on your right.
- (3) Alison was really ***turned off*** by the group of people at the pub, so she left early.

Turn on *(separable):* 1. To start or initiate the operation of something, like a mechanical or electrical device, or start the flow of something, or to switch on, as in this example: *Upon entering the factory, we **turned on** the lights and then turned on the machines.* 2. To leave, divert off of, or move off of a path, road, or route that you had been traveling on and then onto another road, path, route or street, as in this example: *We **turned on** to Queen Street from Cyprus Boulevard.* 3. *(informal)* To excite or interest, , as in this example: *We were really **turned on** by the movie. It was well done.*

More examples:
- (1) It's 8 o'clock in the morning, would you please *turn on* the news.
- (2) Travel down Main Street until you get to 5th Avenue, then *turn onto* 5th Avenue and travel for 5 miles. The library is on your right.
- (3) Alison was really *turned on* by all of the interesting people at the party.

Turn out (inseparable or separable depending on usage): 1. (separable) Similar to turn off, put usually refers to lights, as in this example: *Please turn out the lights when you leave the classroom.* 2. (inseparable) Used to talk about the number of people arriving and being at an event, as in this example: *Many people turned out for the birthday celebration.* 3. (separable) To produce or manufacture, as in this example: *The automobile company turns out thousands of vehicles every year.* 4. (inseparable) To discover that someone or something is a certain way, as in this example: *The student turned out to be a nice person and a hard worker.* 5. (inseparable) To end up, to result in, as in this example: *We didn't think the pizza would be good, but actually the pizza turned out to be delicious.*

More examples:
- (1) We have too many lights on in the house. Please *turn out* the lights in the living room.
- (2) Over 400 people *turned out* for the political meeting.
- (3) The computer company *turns out* thousands of computers every month.

- (4) We thought the policeman was going to me nasty, but he *__turned out__* to be a good guy.
- (5) The cake *__turned out__* good even though we didn't put enough sugar in it.

Turn over (separable): 1. To give something to someone, usually with the meaning to surrender something to someone else, as in this example: *When I left the company, I had to __turn over__ the keys to the office to the boss.* 2. Used to talk about the rate at which employees leave and join a company; when one person leaves a company and a new person is hired, as in this example: *The fast food company __turned over__ its employees very quickly. Sometimes there were two new positions open every week.* 3. To change the position of something so that the bottom becomes the top and the top the bottom, as in this example: *The cook __turned__ the sausages __over__ so that both sides would cook evenly.* 4. Can be used to express the rate of sales of an item, as in this example: *That item __turns over__ very quickly, so it is very important to order more as soon as possible.*

More examples:
- (1) The punishment for drinking and driving is the loss of your driver's license. You have to *__turn__* your license *__over__* to the authorities if you are caught drinking and driving.
- (2) The company was difficult to work for and they *__turned__* their employees *__over__* very quickly.
- (3) When you make pan cakes you have to *__turn__* them *__over__* so that both sides cook.

- (4) The unagi sushi sells very quickly; lots of people buy it and it *turns over* very quickly. Because of this, we have to make a lot of unagi sushi.

Turn up (inseparable or separable depending on usage): 1. (separable) To increase the volume level or level of energy, as in the volume of a radio or other electronic device, as in this example: *I can't hear what they are saying on the TV, could you turn it up?* 2. (inseparable) To show up, appear, to arrive somewhere, as in this example: *A lot of people turned up for the party. I hope we have enough food.*

More examples:
- (1) Please *turn up* the news, that sounds interesting.

(Note: Americans say *turn up* the news, or turn up the announcement when they mean *turn up* the volume of the radio or TV that is playing the news or announcement.)
- (2) Fifteen people *turned up* for the ceremony.

Chapter 12 review
Phrasal verbs beginning with the letter T

Instructions: read and /or listen carefully to the sentences below. Fill in the blank spaces with the correct **preposition, particle,** *or* **adverb**. *The answers can be found in this chapter (above).*

1. My alarm clock stopped working so I took it _____ to see if I could repair it.

2. Fifteen people turned ___ for the ceremony.

3. The company was difficult to work for and they turned their employees ____ very quickly.

4. The cake turned ____ good even though we didn't put enough sugar in it.

5. It's 8 o'clock in the morning, would you please turn ____ the news.

6. The workers tore the roof ____ of the house so that they could put a new one on.

7. She was so angry about her grades that she tore ___ her grades report.

8. I don't taste any difference between this drink and that drink. I can't tell them ____.

9. The salesman wanted to sell me the computer, but I wanted to think ____ it first.

10. The famous actress would sometimes talk _____ to her fans.

11. The tailor took ___ the hem on Jim's new pants.

12. My wife talked me ____ going shopping with her.

13. My boss talked me ____ of quitting my job.

14. If you think _____, you will avoid a lot of problems.

15. Don't quit your job yet. Think it _____, maybe you can find a way to get the things you want at your company.

16. Bridget threw _____ the old batteries and installed new ones in her MP3 player.

17. The woman threw _____ her back when she lifted the child.

18. Alicia was sick all day. She threw ___ twice.

19. The reporter tracked the politician _____ and asked him some questions.

20. The computer store allowed me to trade _____ my old laptop as partial payment for a new one.

Chapter 13
*Phrasal verbs beginning with the letter **U**, **W**, and **Z***

In this section you will learn how to use many different phrasal verbs beginning with the letters U, W, and Z correctly in a sentence.

There are two kinds of phrasal verbs, separable and inseparable. Separable phrasal verbs can take an object between the verb and the preposition. For example: *My father **picked** me **up** after school and drove me home.* Inseparable phrasal verbs cannot take an object between the verb and the preposition. For example: I asked my friends to ***come along*** with me to the Christmas party. ***Come along*** cannot be separated by an object.

The numbers in front of the examples that are in parenthesis (), correspond the to number of the explanation found directly above. So, for example: 1. *explanation* . . . refers to (1) *example* . . . . If there is only one explanation or meaning given for the phrasal verb, then there will be two examples given for the one explanation. Both examples will be marked with (1).

If you have the accompanying Focus on English mp3 audio book (available separately from the school store or from www.FOEBooks.com) listen to each of the phrasal verbs, followed by their meanings and then some examples of how they are used in real English sentences. Each example will be spoken twice. There will be a review at the end of this chapter.

Page 209

There will be a review at the end of this chapter.

Phrasal verbs beginning with the letters U, W, and Z

Read and / or listen carefully to the examples, as they will give you a good idea as to how to use the phrasal verb in real English sentences.

Use up (separable): 1. To exhaust the supply of something, as in this example: *I **used up** all of the milk. Is the store still open? I need to get some milk.*
> **More examples:**
> - (1) I'm tired. I think I've ***used up*** all of my energy.
> - (1) In another 3 miles we will have ***used up*** all of our gas.

Wake up (separable): 1. To awaken, to arouse from sleep, to stop sleeping, as in this example: *I **woke up** at 4 o'clock this morning. I'm really tired.* 2. Sometimes used to express a sudden awareness of something, as in this example: *That exam really **woke** me **up**. I need to study harder.*
> **More examples:**
> - (1) My mother ***woke*** me ***up*** to tell me it was time to get ready for the party.
> - (2) The people keep voting for the wrong leader. They need to ***wake up*** before it is too late.

Warm up (separable): 1. To make warm; usually used to refer to food and drink, but sometimes refers to people and objects, as in this example: *When I came into the house I warmed up a cup of tea.* 2. Sometimes used to express getting more comfortable with someone or something, as in this example: *I warmed up to the new committee and became a member.*

> **More examples:**
> - (1) Would you please *warm up* some coffee for me, I'm late for work.
> - (2) My friend *warmed up* to the idea of playing soccer for another team. He was ready for a change.

Wash off (separable): 1. To remove dirt, soil, or other undesirable marks or contaminants from something, as in this example: *The car was dirty so I washed it off with soap and water.*

> **More examples:**
> - (1) My father *washed* the salt water *off* the boat after fishing all day.
> - (1) I *washed off* my car windshield after the long trip.

Wash up (separable): 1. To clean up, often with soap and water, as in this example: *I washed up the fruit and then put it on the table.* 2. To float onto the shore after being in the water for a period of time, as in this example: *The bottle washed up onto the shore. Inside the bottle there was a message.*

> **More examples:**
> - (1) After dinner, I *washed up* and then went to bed.
> - (2) There is too much pollution that *washes up* onto the shore.

Watch out (inseparable): 1. To be vigilant, alert or aware, as in this example: *Watch out for the bus, it comes this way every hour.* 2. Used to express the need to be cautious or careful, as in this example: *Watch out for falling rocks!*

More examples:
- (1) *Watch out* for the B train, it should be coming through here any moment.
- (2) *Watch out,* don't take another step; there's a snake over there!

Wear down (separable): 1. To breakdown or exhaust by pressure or resistance; become increasingly tired or worn, as in this example: *All of this homework every day is starting to wear me down.* 2. Sometimes used to talk about the process of persuading someone to do or believe something, as in this example: *At first, I didn't want to buy the vacuum cleaner from the salesman, but eventually he wore me down and I bought one.*

More examples:
- (1) John and Naoko drove their car across the United States. When the arrived in California they discovered that they had *worn down* their tires quite a bit.
- (2) Our daughter wanted to stay out late but we didn't think it was a good idea. She asked us many times during the day if she could stay out late and eventually she *wore* us *down* and we said yes.

Wear off (inseparable): 1. When the effect of something gradually diminishes or gets smaller, as in this example: *The effects of the alcohol gradually wore off.*
   More examples:
   - (1) When the drug *wore off*, I really felt pain.
   - (1) I drank too much coffee. I was glad when the effects of the caffeine finally *wore off*.

Wear out (separable): 1. To become or to cause something to become unusable or weak, as in this example: *I wore out the brakes in my car by traveling down steep hills and mountains.* 2. To become tired, as in this example: *We played soccer all afternoon. We really wore ourselves out.*
   More examples:
   - (1) I have to get a new CD player. I *wore out* the old one by playing it so much.
   - (2) Grandfather had to take a nap. His grandchildren *wore* him *out* playing in the yard.

Wind up (separable or inseparable depending on usage): 1. (inseparable) Similar to end up or finish up; to experience the results or consequence of something because of something you did, as in this example: *We took the wrong road to town and wound up in a place we weren't familiar with.* 2. (separable) Similar to wrap up; to take the necessary action to complete something or to cause to come to the end of something, as in this example: *We wound up our meeting by shaking hands.* 3. (separable) To turn the key or handle on something that is usually attached to a spring, like in a child's toy car, as in this example: *The boy <u>wound up</u> his little toy car and then put it on the ground and watched it race away.* 4. (separable) To wrap something like rope, line or tape around something like a cylinder or other object, as in this example: *After we flew the kite, we <u>wound up</u> the string and went home.* 5. (inseparable) In baseball, when the pitcher prepare to throw a ball at the batter, as in this example: *The pitcher <u>wound up</u> and then threw a fast ball at the batter.*

    More examples:
- (1) I didn't study for the exam and <u>*wound up*</u> getting a failing grade.
- (2) Our team <u>*wound up*</u> the game with a winning goal.
- (3) My friend had an old watch that had to be <u>*wound up*</u> in order for it to continue to work.
- (4) The sailor <u>*wound*</u> the line <u>*up*</u> around a post on the ship.
- (5) The pitcher <u>*wound up*</u> and threw a curve ball.

<u>Wipe off</u> (separable): 1. To clean a surface; to remove liquid, dirt, dust or other material from a surface, as in this example: *After we finished dinner, I <u>wiped off</u> the table.*

    More examples:
- (1) After traveling through the dusty countryside, I <u>*wiped*</u> the dust <u>*off*</u> the car.
- (2) We cleaned up the bedroom yesterday. We vacuumed the floor and <u>*wiped off*</u> the shelves.

Wipe up (separable): 1. Usually used to mean a brief cleaning up; sometimes when you spill liquid you wipe it up; to clean up here and there, as in this example: *After feeding the baby, the mother had to wipe up around the baby's table.*
- More examples:
  - (1) These vinyl seats are easy to take care of. If you spill something on them all you have to do is *wipe* it *up* with a clean towel.
  - (1) We *wiped up* the kitchen after breakfast and then went to the beach.

Work in(to) (separable): 1. To introduce or insert something or someone into something else like a conversation, a plan, project, or activity, as in this example: *We have to find a way to work John into the plan.* (Meaning: We have to find a way to use or let John participate in our plan) 2. To make an opening in a schedule for someone, as in this example: *The doctor's secretary worked the sick woman into the doctor's schedule.* 3. To insert or fit by repeatedly and continuously moving something around into something else; to jiggle something to get it into something else, as in this example: *He worked the old key into the lock.* (Meaning: The word 'jiggle' means to move something quickly from side to side.)
- More examples:
  - (1) We like your idea and we are going to try to *work* it *into* our project.

- (2) The teacher was very busy, but was kind enough to *work* me *into* his schedule so we could discuss my exam.
- (3) The fisherman carefully *worked* his hook *into* the bait.

Work out (separable): 1. Used to talk about being successful at something, as in this example: *We sold our home and bought another home that was more beautiful. We're glad now that we sold the old house and bought the new house. It really worked out well.* 2. To solve something or to find a solution for something, as in this example: *The student worked out the math problem.* 3. Used to talk about a specific result, as in this example: *The answer to the formula worked out to be 25.* 4. To participate in strenuous exercise or physical conditioning, as in this example: *I worked out at the gym every night.*

More examples:
- (1) Studying every night for that exam *worked out* perfectly. I got a 97%.
- (2) At first, our group could not agree on a name for our new company, but we finally *worked* it *out*.
- (3) It *worked out* that we all fit on the same bus. We didn't have to take separate buses to the museum.
- (4) If you want to be an Olympic athlete, you have to *work out* hard.

Work up (inseparable): 1. To cause to be anxious, excited or emotional about something or someone; to arouse the emotions or to excite, as in this example: *My sister's best friend was injured* *in a car accident. My sister is all <u>worked up</u> about it.* 2. To build proficiency, skill, responsibility or status through work, as in this example: *Jim <u>worked</u> his way <u>up</u> to vice president of the company.* 3. To build or develop something over time as a result of effort or work, as in this example: *We played soccer all morning. We're hungry. We really <u>worked up</u> an appetite for lunch.*

> **More examples:**
> - (1) What's wrong with Klaus? He's all <u>worked up</u> because he didn't get a good grade on the final exam.
> 1. (2) Shohei worked hard in his company. He <u>worked</u> his way <u>up</u> to manager in just one year.
> - (3) I spent the whole day at the beach and really <u>worked up</u> a thirst. I could drink a gallon of water right now!

Wrap up (separable): 1. To complete something, finish with something or bring something to a conclusion, as in this example: *The teacher <u>wrapped up</u> the class promptly at 2pm.* 2. To cover something with gift wrap, paper, packaging paper or other kind of wrapper, as in this example: *I <u>wrapped up</u> the gifts that I will give my sister on her birthday.* 3. To summarize, as in this example: *The teacher <u>wrapped up</u> the class by going over the main points of the lesson.*

> **More examples:**
> - (1) We <u>wrapped up</u> the business meeting at 10 o'clock.
> - (2) Janice <u>wrapped up</u> her sister's gift the day before the party.

❑ (3) The manager *wrapped up* the business meeting with a brief discussion of our latest sales information.

Write down (*separable*): 1. To write or set something on paper, as in this example: *As I gave her my phone number, she wrote it down on paper.*
> **More examples:**
> ❑ (1) The students *wrote down* everything the teacher said..
> ❑ (1) The police officer *wrote down* my address.

Write up (*separable*): 1. To document something; to write a report or description of, like for a publication, as in this example: *News of the event was written up in the newspaper.* 2. To report in writing, like when you break the law for speeding etc., as in this example: *The policeman wrote the woman up for going to fast.*
> **More examples:**
> ❑ (1) The idea for the compressed air motor was *written up* in the auto magazine.
> ❑ (2) Kimberly crossed the street while the light was still red. A policeman caught her and *wrote* her *up* for crossing the street against the red light.

Zip up (*separable*): 1. To close up an opening, usually in clothing or cloth goods, using a zipper, as in this example: *I zipped up my jacket and left the building.*
> **More examples:**
> ❑ (1) Mom, would you help me *zip up* my dress?

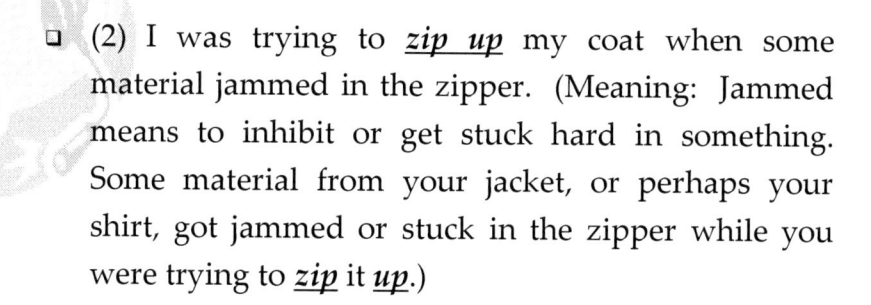

❏ (2) I was trying to *zip up* my coat when some material jammed in the zipper. (Meaning: Jammed means to inhibit or get stuck hard in something. Some material from your jacket, or perhaps your shirt, got jammed or stuck in the zipper while you were trying to *zip* it *up*.)

Chapter 13 review

*Phrasal verbs beginning with the letters **U**, **W**, and **Z***

*Instructions: read and /or listen carefully to the sentences below. Fill in the blank spaces with the correct **preposition, particle,** or **adverb**. The answers can be found in this chapter (above).*

1. We like your idea and we are going to try to work it ____ our project.

2. It worked ____ that we all fit on the same bus. We didn't have to take separate buses to the museum.

3. I spent the whole day at the beach and really worked ____ a thirst. I could drink a gallon of water right now!

4. Mom, would you help me zip ____ my dress?

5. The idea for the compressed air motor was written ____ in the auto magazine.

6. Janice wrapped ____ her sister's gift the day before the party.

7. We wiped ___ the kitchen after breakfast and then went to the beach.

8. After traveling through the dusty countryside, I wiped the dust ___ the car.

9. I didn't study for the exam and wound ___ getting a failing grade.

10. When the drug wore ___, I really felt pain.

11. I washed ___ my car windshield after the long trip.

12. Would you please warm ___ some coffee for me, I'm late for work.

13. My mother woke me ___ to tell me it was time to get ready for the party.

14. I'm tired. I think I've used ___ all of my energy.

15. John and Naoko drove their car across the United States. When the arrived in California they discovered that they had worn ___ their tires quite a bit.

INDEX

Chapter 1

- aim at, 2
- ask for, 2
- ask out, 2
- ask over, 3
- back down, 3
- back off, 3
- back up, 4
- beat up, 4
- beef up, 4
- believe in, 5
- bite off, 5
- blow away, 5
- blow off, 6
- blow out, 7
- blow up, 7
- boil down to, 7
- break down, 8
- break in, 9
- break off, 9
- break out, 10
- break through, 10
- break up, 11
- bring back, 11
- bring over, 11
- bring up, 12
- brush up, 12
- brush off, 12
- build in, 13
- bump into, 13
- burn down, 13
- burn up, 14
- burst out, 14
- butt in, 15

Chapter 2

- call back, 19
- call in, 19
- call off, 20
- call up, 20

Page 222

INDEX

- calm down, 21
- care for, 21
- carry on, 21
- carry out, 22
- catch on, 22
- catch up, 22
- cheat on, 23
- check in, 24
- check out, 24
- chop up, 24
- clean out, 25
- clear up, 25
- clog up, 25
- close off, 26
- come across, 26
- come along, 26
- come apart, 27
- come back, 27
- come down, 28
- come down with, 28
- come from, 29

- come in, 29
- come off, 30
- come on, 30
- come out, 31
- come through, 31
- come up, 32
- come up with, 32
- con into, 33
- con out of, 33
- cool off, 33
- count in, 34
- count on, 34
- count up, 34
- cover up, 35
- crack down, 35
- cross off, 36
- cut back, 36
- cut down, 36
- cut off, 37
- cut out, 38
- cut up, 38

Chapter 3

Page 223

INDEX

- deal with, 42
- do away with, 42
- do over, 43
- do without, 43
- dress up, 44
- drink down, 44
- drink up, 44
- drop in, 45
- drop off, 45
- drop out, 45
- dry off, 46
- dry out, 46
- dry up, 47
- eat up, 47
- eat out, 48
- empty out, 48
- end up, 49
- fall apart, 48
- fall behind, 49
- fall down, 49
- fall for, 49

- fall off, 50
- fall out, 50
- fall over, 51
- fall through, 52
- feel up to, 52
- fight back, 52
- figure on, 53
- figure out, 53
- fill in, 53
- fill out, 54
- fill up, 54
- find out, 55
- fix up, 55
- flip out, 56
- float around, 56
- follow through, 56
- follow up, 57
- fool around, 57
- freak out, 58

Chapter 4

- get ahead, 62
- get along, 62

INDEX

- get around to, 63
- get away, 63
- get back, 64
- get back at, 64
- get back to, 65
- get behind, 65
- get by, 65
- get down, 66
- get in, 66
- get off, 67
- get off on, 67
- get on, 68
- get out, 68
- get out of, 69
- get over, 70
- get over with, 70
- get through, 70
- get to, 71
- get together, 71
- get up, 72
- give away, 72
- give back, 73
- give in, 73
- give out, 74
- give up, 74

- go about, 75
- go after, 75
- go ahead, 75
- go along with, 76
- go around, 76
- go away, 77
- go back, 77
- go back on, 77
- go beyond, 78
- go by, 78
- go down, 79
- go for, 79
- go in, 80
- go off, 80
- go on, 81
- go out, 82
- go over, 82
- go through, 83
- go up, 83
- go with, 84
- goof around, 84
- gross out, 84
- grow out (of), 85
- grow up, 85

Page 225

INDEX

Chapter 5

- hand back, 89
- hand in, 89
- hand out, 89
- hand over, 90
- hang around, 90
- hang on, 90
- hang out, 91
- hang up, 91
- have on, 91
- head back, 92
- head for, 92
- head off, 92
- head towards, 93

- hear about, 93
- hear of, 93
- heat up, 94
- help out, 94
- hit on, 94
- hold against, 95
- hold off, 95
- hold on, 95
- hold out, 96
- hold over, 96
- hold up, 97
- hook up, 97
- hurry up, 98

Chapter 6

- keep at, 102
- keep away, 102
- keep down, 102
- keep from, 103
- keep off, 103
- keep on, 103
- keep to, 104

- keep up, 104
- kick back, 105
- kick out, 105
- knock off, 106
- knock out, 106
- knock over, 107
- know about, 108

INDEX

Chapter 7

- lay down, 111
- lay off, 111
- lead up to, 112
- leave behind, 112
- leave off, 113
- leave out, 113
- let down, 113
- let in, 114
- let in on, 114
- let off, 114
- let out, 115
- let up, 115
- lie around, 116
- lie down, 116
- lift up, 116
- light up, 117

- line up, 117
- live with, 118
- lock in, 118
- lock out, 118
- lock up, 119
- look around, 119
- look at, 120
- look down on, 120
- look for, 121
- look forward to, 121
- look into, 121
- look out, 122
- look over, 122
- look up, 122
- look up to, 122
- luck out, 123

Chapter 8

- make for, 127
- make of, 127
- make out, 128
- make up, 128

- mess up, 129
- mix up, 129
- move in, 130
- move out, 130

INDEX

- narrow down, 130
- open up, 131

Chapter 9

- pass on, 134
- pass out, 134
- pass over, 134
- pass up, 135
- pay back, 135
- pay for, 135
- pay off, 136
- pay up, 136
- pick on, 136
- pick out, 137
- pick up, 137
- pile up, 139
- piss off, 139
- plan ahead, 139
- plan for, 140
- plan on, 140
- play around, 140
- plug in, 141
- plug up, 141
- point out, 142
- point to, 142
- print out, 143
- pull off, 143
- pull out, 143
- pull over, 144
- pull through, 144
- punch in, 144
- punch out, 145
- put away, 145
- put back, 145
- put down, 146
- put in, 147
- put off, 148
- put on, 148
- put out, 149
- put past, 149
- put to, 150
- put together, 150
- put up, 151
- put up with, 152

INDEX

Chapter 10

- rip off, 156
- rip up, 156
- rule out, 157
- run across, 157
- run around, 157
- run down, 158
- run into, 158
- run out, 159
- run over, 159
- run up, 160

Chapter 11

- screw on, 163
- screw out of, 163
- screw up, 164
- see about, 164
- sell out, 165
- set out, 165
- set up, 166
- settle down, 166
- settle for, 167
- shake off, 167
- shake up, 168
- show off, 168
- show up, 169
- shut off, 169
- shut up, 170
- sign in, 170
- sign out, 171
- sign up, 171
- sit down, 171
- slip up, 172
- slow down, 172
- sneak in, 173
- sneak out, 173
- sort out, 174
- space out, 174
- stand around, 174
- stand for, 175
- stand up, 175
- start off, 176
- start out, 176

INDEX

- start over, 177
- start up, 177
- stay off, 177
- stay out, 178
- stay up, 178
- step on, 179
- stick around, 179
- stick out, 179
- stick to, 180

- stick up, 180
- stick with, 181
- stop off, 182
- stop over, 182
- straighten out, 183
- straighten up, 183
- stress out, 184
- switch off, 184
- switch on, 184

Chapter 12

- take apart, 188
- take in, 188
- take off, 190
- take on, 191
- take out, 191
- take out (on), 191
- take over, 192
- Take to, 192
- take up, 193
- talk down (to), 194
- talk into, 194
- talk out of, 194
- tear down, 195

- tear off, 195
- tear up, 195
- tell apart, 196
- think about, 196
- think ahead, 197
- think over, 197
- throw away, 197
- throw out, 198
- throw up, 198
- track down, 199
- trade in, 199
- trick into, 200
- try on, 200

INDEX

- try out, 200
- turn around, 201
- turn down, 201
- turn in, 202
- turn into, 202

- turn off, 203
- turn on, 203
- turn out, 204
- turn over, 205
- turn up, 206

Chapter 13

- use up, 210
- wake up, 210
- warm up, 211
- wash off, 211
- wash up, 211
- watch out, 212
- wear down, 212
- wear off, 213
- wear out, 213
- wind up, 213

- wipe off, 214
- wipe up, 215
- work in, 215
- work out, 216
- work up, 216
- wrap up, 217
- write down, 218
- write up, 218
- zip up, 218

NOTES

NOTES